THE ILLUSTRATED CATALOG OF

GUITARS

THE ILLUSTRATED CATALOG OF GUITARS

250 AMAZING MODELS FROM ACOUSTIC TO ELECTRIC

NICK FREETH

Skyhorse Publishing

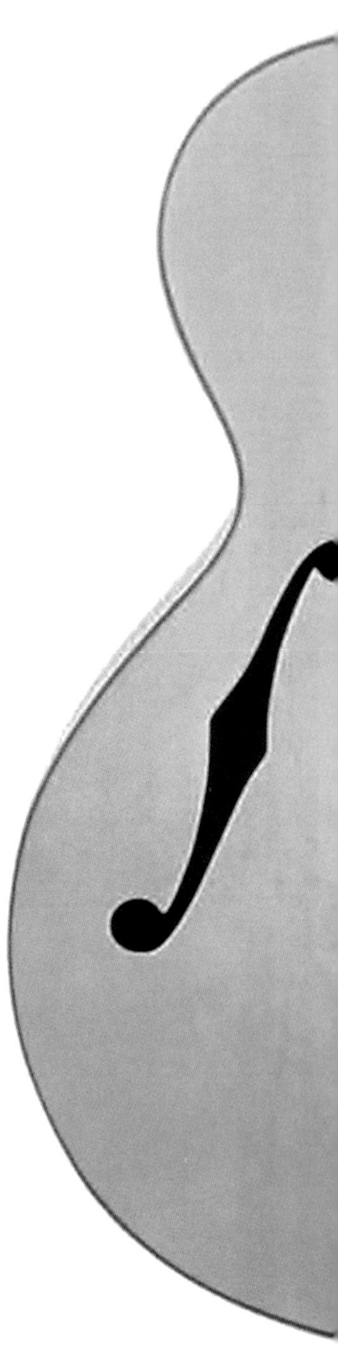

Copyright © 2009, 2010, 2022 by Nick Freeth

First published by Pepperbox Press, 2009, 2010

First Skyhorse Publishing Edition 2022

All rights reserved. No part of this book may be reproduced in any manner without the express written consent of the publisher, except in the case of brief excerpts in critical reviews or articles. All inquiries should be addressed to Skyhorse Publishing, 307 West 36th Street, 11th Floor, New York, NY 10018.

Skyhorse Publishing books may be purchased in bulk at special discounts for sales promotion, corporate gifts, fund-raising, or educational purposes. Special editions can also be created to specifications. For details, contact the Special Sales Department, Skyhorse Publishing, 307 West 36th Street, 11th Floor, New York, NY 10018 or info@skyhorsepublishing.com.

Skyhorse® and Skyhorse Publishing® are registered trademarks of Skyhorse Publishing, Inc.®, a Delaware corporation.

Visit our website at www.skyhorsepublishing.com.

10 9 8 7 6 5 4 3 2 1

Library of Congress Cataloging-in-Publication Data is available on file.

Cover design by David Ter-Avanesyan
Cover photo credit: Getty Images

Paperback ISBN: 978-1-5107-5654-0
Ebook ISBN: 978-1-5107-5681-6

Printed in China

CONTENTS

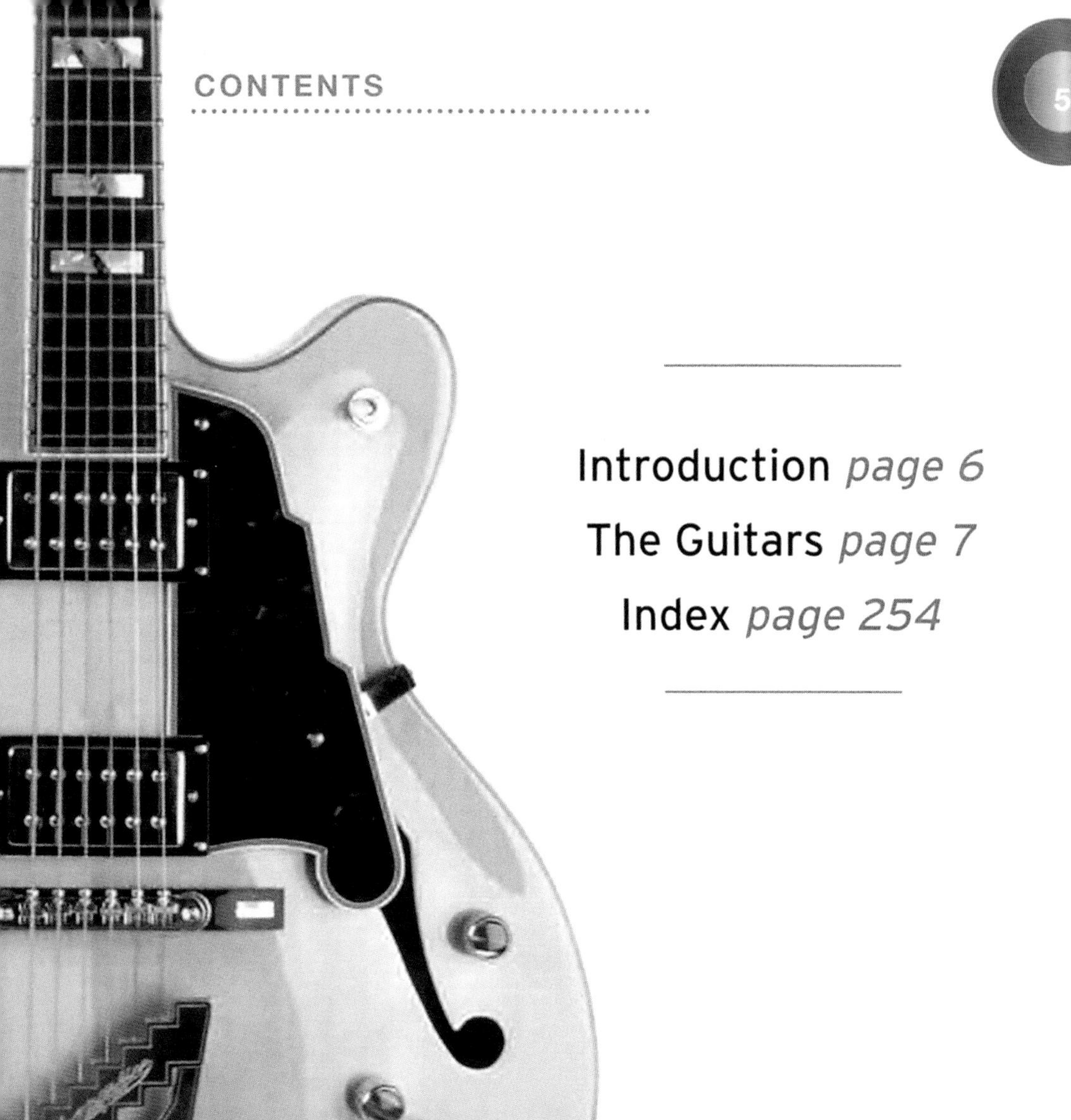

Introduction

The art of guitar design has evolved rapidly over the past 80 years, from the acoustic, arch-topped Gibson L-5 in the early 1920s, through the solid-bodied Fender models of the 1950s and 60s, to the exoskeletal construction, comprising carbon and glass fiber, of the Parker Fly in the 1990s. Such leaps of style and period are, of course, inevitable in a book of this kind, but their ultimate effect is to remind us of the similarities that unite even the most sharply contrasting guitars featured here.

All were intended to produce sounds satisfying to musicians and their audiences; all were made using a combination of technical skill, artistic imagination, and practical purpose; and all can be appreciated both for their craftsmanship and their more intangible ability to inspire and excite.

Just as automobiles, in the early years, retained the shape of the horse drawn carriage, so too did guitars reflect the design of earlier instruments like violins and mandolins. The Gibson L-5 ''Master Model'' of 1922 is a prime example, taking its cue from the company's acclaimed mandolin designs.

However as advances in electronics did away with the absolute necessity of a sound-projecting hollow body, designers had the freedom to experiment with solid instruments, such as those developed by Leo Fender in the early 1950s.

Appearance too, from the 1950s onward, became a significant factor in guitar design. Rock and Roll stars wanted to look cool with a really hot-looking instrument dangling from their hip, and so the race was on to produce models that reflected contemporary youth style and culture.

Soon, guitar models bearing the names of famous players began to appear: notable examples have included Gibson's *Everly Brothers* acoustics, The Mosrite *Ventures*, Fender's custom *Eric Clapton* Stratocaster, and [more recently] the Dean *Dimebag* Tribute ML.

The circumstances and methods of guitars' creation vary widely-but characters as apparently disparate as Orville Gibson, hand crafting his groundbreaking archtops at his Kalamazoo, Michigan workshop in the early 1900s, and Leo Fender, endlessly striking heavily amplified open strings in his office in California in the 1950s, shared many of the same goals, and have a great deal more in common than is sometimes believed.

We have carefully picked the selection of instruments in this book to reflect the evolution of the guitar, organized alphabetically for quick reference.

We hope you will enjoy reading it, either by dipping in, or cover-to-cover!

Alembic Entwistle Bass

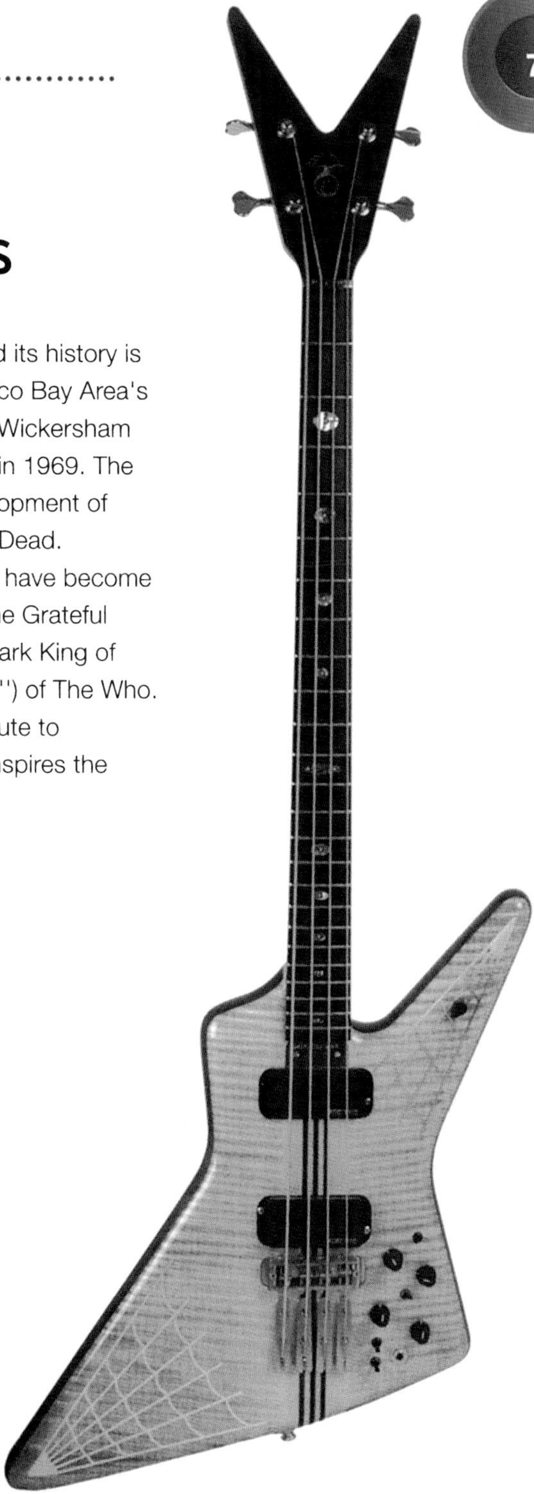

Alembic is based in Santa Rosa, California, and its history is closely intertwined with that of the San Francisco Bay Area's rich rock music scene. Electronics expert Ron Wickersham and his artist wife Susan formed the company in 1969. The company quickly became involved in the development of custom-built gear for members of the Grateful Dead.

Alembic's technically innovative instruments have become the choice of many leading performers, from the Grateful Dead's Phil Lesh to jazzman Stanley Clarke, Mark King of Level 42, and the late John Entwistle (''The Ox'') of The Who. The ''Spyder'' basses were produced as a tribute to Entwistle. His famous song Boris the Spider' inspires the name.

Alembic's logo, designed by Bob Thomas in 1969, incorporates a number of astrological and mystic symbols.

Alembic Dragon Bass

The Who's John Entwistle also has a connection with the Alembic Dragon bass shown on this page. It was inspired by a design originally conceived by Susan Wickersham for a custom Entwistle model with (as she puts it) "a dragon's wing for a body and a dragon's claw for a peghead."

Like nearly all the Alembics, the guitar makes use of Ron Wickersham's unique pickup circuitry. The bass's so-called "Signature"-type electronics include volume and pan knobs, and two filter controls, one associated with each pickup. The provision of such "tailoring tools" is central to Alembic's philosophy, which its co-founder Ron Wickersham summed up to this author in The Electric Guitar.

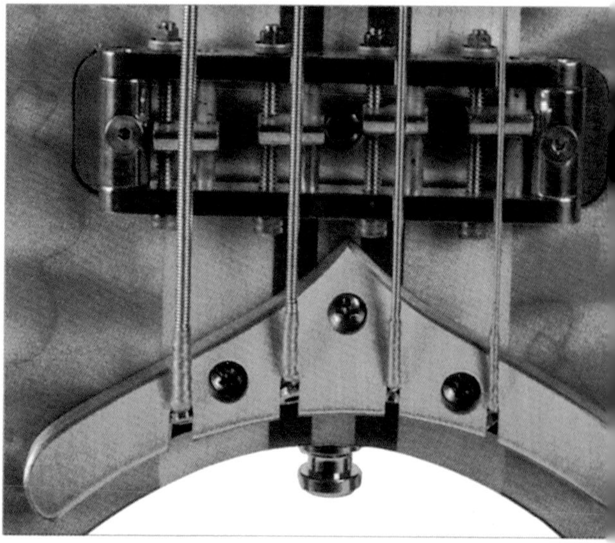

The heavy-duty bridge and tailpiece fitted to the Dragon Bass are machined out of solid brass.

Alembic Tribute

Jerry Garcia (1945-1995) lead guitarist and frontman for the Grateful Dead used a wide range of electric instruments during his extraordinary career. He started out with a Danelectro, and was subsequently seen with a Guild Starfire, Gibson SGs and Les Pauls, and a Fender Stratocaster, as well as some more unusual models, such as the aluminum-necked Travis Beans he sported in the 1970s.

Doug Irwin, a former Alembic staffer, also built Garcia no less than five custom electrics for him. Alembic has now produced a Garcia Tribute instrument. The guitar has a multi-ply body, typically flexible Alembic electronics, and its ebony-faced headstock is graced with a sterling silver-inlaid company logo.

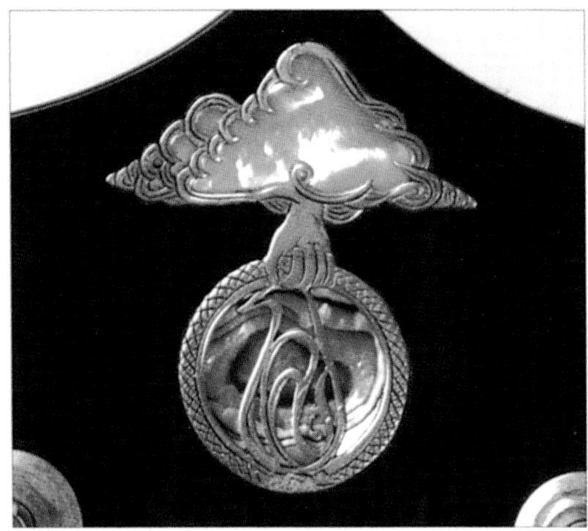

Alembic explains its mystical logo thus: "Mankind takes everything in the universe and in an infinite search for wisdom, focuses energy into the alembic resulting in the purest goal."

Alembic Orion Baritone Guitar

For players accompanying deep-voiced singers, or seeking an alternative timbre to that of a conventional instrument, a baritone guitar, which is usually tuned a perfect fourth or fifth lower than its standard counterpart, can be a pleasing choice. Quite a number of acoustic and electronic baritones are now available, and Alembic's Orion model is among the finest around. Its shape is broadly similar to that of Alembic's EADGBE-tuned and bass Orions. Like its higher-pitched 6-string sister, it has a mahogany body, which is then given a top made from a choice of exotic woods. In this case, the hardwood coco bolo. But at 28 inches, the Orion's scale is 2½ inches longer than a standard guitar's.

Tom Anderson Hollow Drop Top

A keen guitarist from the age of eight, Tom Anderson spent several years as a professional musician before becoming involved in designing, maintaining, and modifying instruments. Between 1977 and 1984, he worked at Schecter, before setting up his own, California-based company. Launched in 1991, the Drop Top (whose name refers to the instruments maple or koa upper surface, molded over a basswood or alder body) is one of Anderson's enduring classics.

This one is the "Hollow Drop Top," which contains sealed chambers to add richness to the guitar's tone. Its rich purple is complemented by the instrument's chromed hardware, including a "vintage tremolo."

Anderson's trademark: the company describes itself as "dedicated to creating the world's finest feeling, playing, and sounding guitars."

Tom Anderson Cobra Special

Tom Anderson's Cobra line of electrics began in 1993 with the original, maple-topped mahogany Cobra. This was a single cutaway model, fitted with two powerful humbucking pickups, and featured the company's usual comprehensive switching options. Cobras with chambered bodies soon followed.

The Cobra Special is among the later incarnations of the instrument. According to the company's 1998 catalog, Tom Anderson himself felt that this stylish instrument was best suited to his own playing style. This example is finished in "TV Yellow." "Translucent Cherry" and several alternative colors are also available. The Special has a bolted-on maple neck, and has a scale length of 24¾ inches.

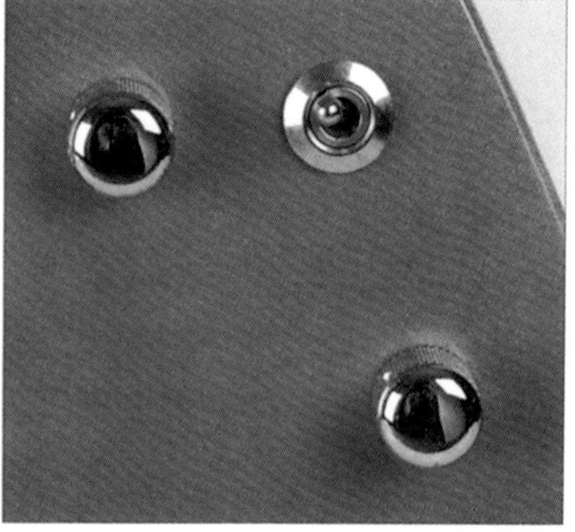

The volume control knobs and pickup selector switch, like the rest of the Cobra Special's hardware, is reassuringly chunky.

Tom Anderson Atom

Tom Anderson has been a devotee of bolted-on electric guitar necks for many years. But in 2005, Anderson announced a completely new model, the Atom, which used a completely innovative neck joint, described as "a three-dimensional trapezoidal wedge." The joint is said to offer unrivalled rigidity and alignment. The instrument also has several other novel features including a wraparound bridge and a body shape that was new to Anderson.

Different numbers and types of pickups, alternative woods, and differing nut widths are also available. This model has a quilted maple top, finished in "Deep Ocean Blue," laid over a mahogany body. Its neck is also mahogany.

Dan Armstrong Lucite Bass

Dan Armstrong (1934-2004) started out as a professional guitarist, but later switched to designing, repairing, and modifying instruments at his workshop in New York City. In 1968, his "see through" electric guitars and basses, with bodies of transparent Lucite and bolted-on maple necks, were put into production by the New Jersey-based Ampeg company.

Dense, easy to work with, and strongly resistant to damage and vibration, Lucite seemed the ideal material for solid electrics. Both Keith Richards of the Rolling Stones and Jack Bruce of Cream are known to have played these instruments. Ampeg stopped making these intriguing guitars in 1971, but briefly revived them in the late 1990s.

This late 1960s model carries the autograph of celebrity Armstrong user Jack Bruce of Cream.

Art & Lutherie Cedar Cutaway

Art & Lutherie (which designs and manufactures in La Patrie, Canada) is the brainchild of Robert Godin. Godin is the creator of many major guitar brands, including Godin itself, and Norman. Art & Lutherie was founded to produce what Godin describes as "entry-level acoustics that would bring the key attributes of pro-quality [instruments] within the reach of novice players."

High-tech developments in manufacturing have helped to bring about dramatic improvements in the once dire quality of many inexpensive flat-tops, but Art & Lutherie models, such as the Cedar Cutaway, are among the very best. This modestly priced guitar has a solid top, a pleasing sound, and easy action.

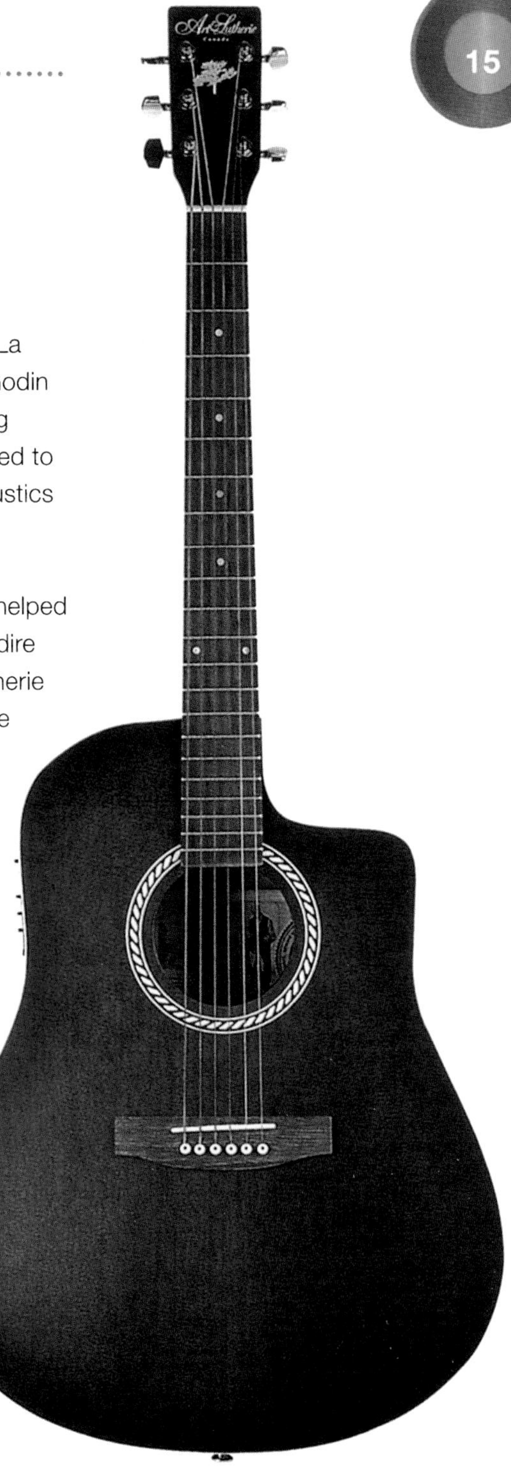

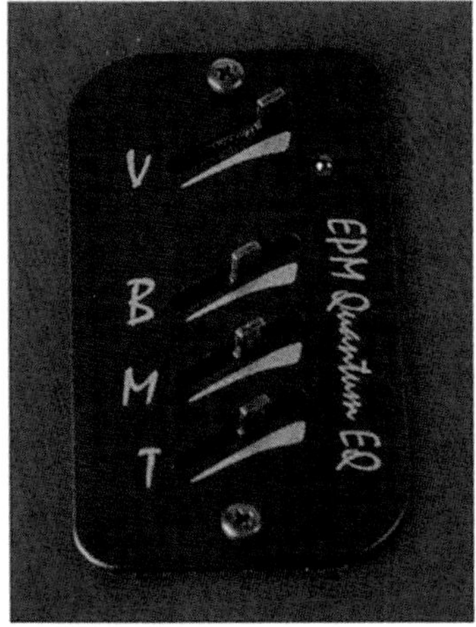

Pickup systems are now commonly found on cheaper acoustics. This preamp unit is simple, but effective.

Benedetto Bucky Pizzarelli

Robert Benedetto is widely acknowledged as the greatest of all living archtop guitar makers. Craftsmanship runs in his family: he learned his woodworking skills from his father and grandfather, who were both cabinet-makers. Bob began his own lutherie career in the late 1960s.

For many years, he combined instrument building with repair and restoration work to make ends meet. However, the quality of his guitars gradually gained recognition, and in 1978, he received a commission for a 7-stringer from jazzman Bucky Pizzarelli. This example was made recently at Fender, under Benedetto's supervision.

From 1999 until 2006, Benedetto guitars were built by Fender.

Benedetto Bravo

Since Robert Benedetto built his 7-string guitar for Bucky Pizzarelli, many other prominent players, including the late Chuck Wayne, Kenny Burrell, Jimmy Bruno, and British jazzman Martin Taylor, have adopted his instruments. Benedetto has also made a number of violins and cellos.

Benedettos tend to be lighter, and often slightly narrower, than many earlier American archtops; Bob believes that, ''big isn't necessarily better or louder.'' In 1999, Bob began to work with Fender, and this Bravo was one of the fruits of this partnership, that came to an end in 2006. Benedetto now plans to establish its own manufacturing facility in Savannah, Georgia.

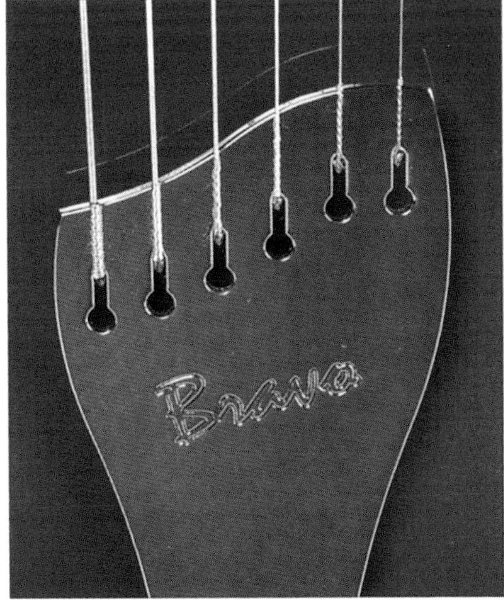

The gold-plated tailpiece nicely compliments the Bravo's ''Claret'' coloring.

Blueridge Historic Series BR-163CE

Blueridge flat-tops are manufactured for Saga Musical Instruments. Based in San Francisco, the company is one of America's leading importers of guitars, violins, and mandolins. Musician and storekeeper Richard Keldsen founded Saga in the mid-1970s. Its first products were made in Japan, but the company now manufactures in China.

Thanks to careful design and meticulous quality control, the results of this collaboration have been outstanding. This 000-sized BR-163 (one of the Blueridge "Historic Series") offers exceptional quality at a competitive price. The model sports a high gloss finish on its solid Sitka spruce top. Its back, sides, and bridge are made from Indian rosewood.

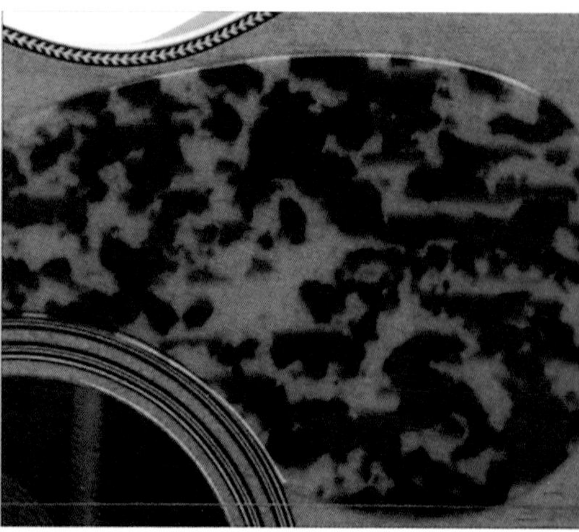

Detail of the pickguard and herringbone inlay, which was inspired by 1930s Martin guitars.

Bourgeois DS-260

Dana Bourgeois comes from Maine. He made his first acoustic guitar while a student at Bowdoin College in Brunswick, and became a professional luthier in 1978. In 1995, Bourgeois established his own company, Bourgeois Guitars, in Lewiston, Maine. Although few in number, his instruments were soon adopted by several leading players, including Ricky Skaggs and Steve Earle. This Bourgeois DS-260 production model dates from 1997. One commentator praised its "lovely warm, balanced tone." Bourgeois made fewer than 100 DS-260s, but the guitar is now being constructed in larger numbers by Pantheon, a new company co-founded by Dana Bourgeois in 2000.

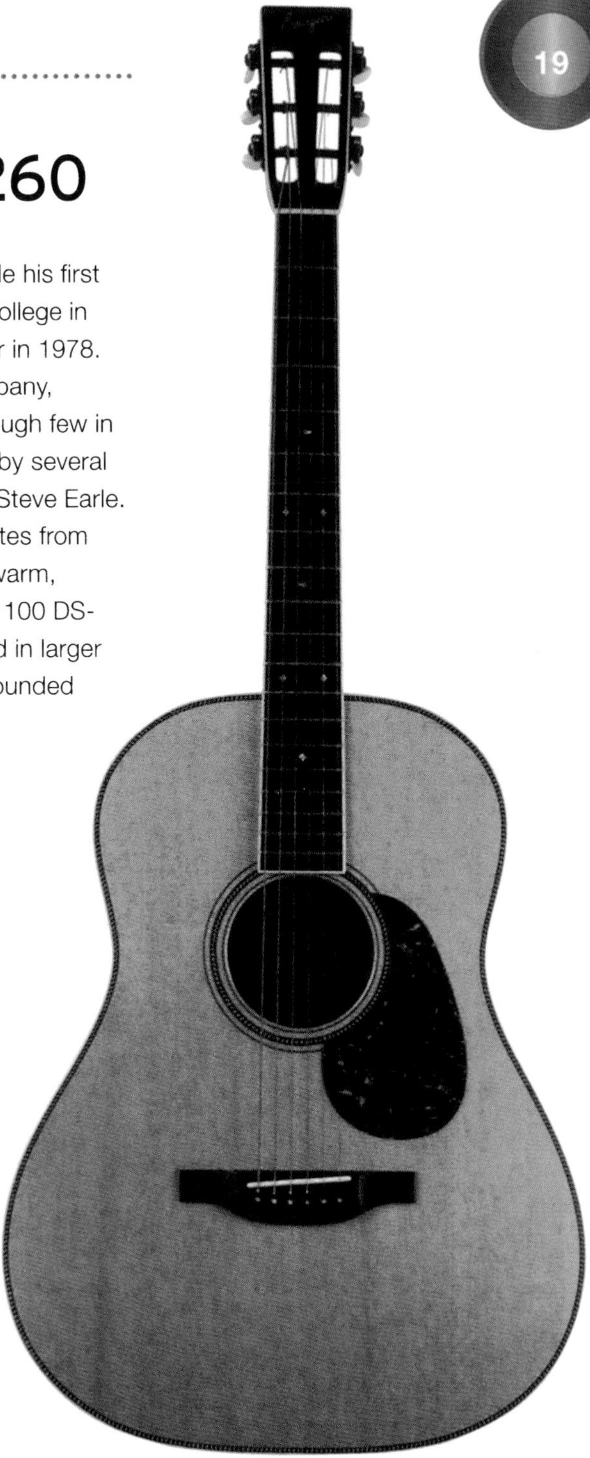

Breedlove D 20

Larry Breedlove and Steve Henderson founded the Breedlove Guitar Company, based near Bend, Oregon, in 1990. Originally from California, both men had worked for the area's most famous guitar maker, Bob Taylor, before decided to strike our on their own. Larry was responsible for creating two of the most distinctive features associated with Breedlove flat-tops: their sharp cutaways and arrowed headstocks.

Demand for the company's instruments soon grew, and Larry's brother, Kim, (a banjo maker) joined the staff. He now part-owns the company, and is its master luthier. This recently made Breedlove D20 is a Dreadnought model, popular with flatpickers and bluegrass players.

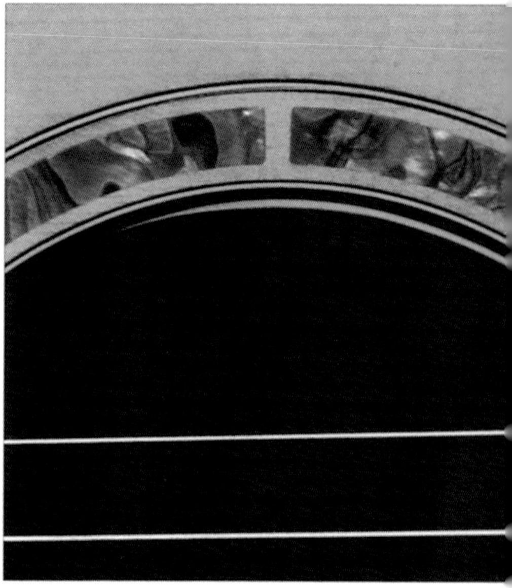

Breedlove SC 25

In its early days, Breedlove employed only a handful of craftsmen, but has subsequently expanded both its staff and its product lines. Company president Peter Newport and master luthier Kim Breedlove are both keen to offer Breedlove customers affordable flat-tops as well as deluxe and custom models.

To this end, the company introduced its "S" (for "simplified") series. These guitars still feature premium tonewoods, meticulous design, and masterly construction. The featured guitar is a "simplified concert" model, with black bindings, a 15-inch maximum body width, and company co-founder, Steve Henderson's "soft" cutaway design.

Fishman preamps are factory fitted to many Breedlove SC 25s.

Burns Marvin Shadows Custom

Jim Burns (1925-1998), sometimes hailed as the "British Leo Fender," was an able guitarist who acquired craft and metalworking skills while serving as a Royal Air Force fitter during World War II, and soon applied them to instrument making.

In 1959, his solid-body designs became commercially available for the first time. In 1963, Burns persuaded Hank Marvin, lead guitarist with one of the United Kingdom's most prominent pop groups, The Shadows, and previously a dedicated Fender Stratocaster user, to collaborate with him on a Burns electric carrying his endorsement.
The Burns Marvin debuted in 1964. Now made in China, the guitar has an alder body and maple neck.

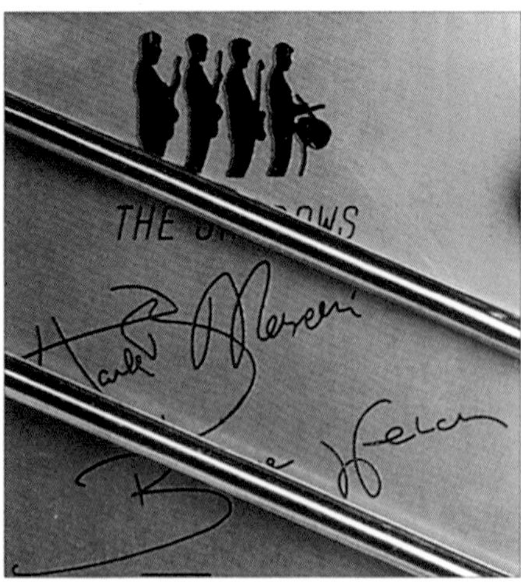

The signatures of Hank B. Marvin and Bruce Welch appear on the "Rezo-Tube" vibrato of this special edition guitar.

Burns Marquee

In 1999, Burns London introduced a range of instruments built in the Far East to its own specifications. The first of these was the Marquee, a budget-priced, three-pickup solid inspired by the Burns Legend, itself a replica of the Marvin Shadows Custom. This Marquee is finished in "Shadows White;" its other available colors include "Jet Black" (named for Shadows' bassist Jet Harris). The bodies of earlier Marquees were made from alder, but Burns has now switched to agathis wood (sourced from a rainforest conifer).

Flamed maple is used for the Marquee's 22-fret neck. Since its introduction, the Marquee has won over a growing number of critics and players in Britain and the United States.

Chanticleer O/R

Patrick Arbuthnot, a British luthier who served an apprenticeship as a sheet-metal worker in the early 1970s before becoming a professional musician, made this single-resonator guitar. Playing both regular and steel guitar, he went on to tour and record extensively, appearing throughout North America. It was while performing that Patrick decided he needed a louder acoustic instrument, and built himself a resonator-equipped mandolin.

He was soon producing other, similar models, which delivered the sonic power he sought. Working for an airplane restoration company led him to adopt "a more industrial appearance." Patrick now trades as Chanticleer Resonator Instruments.

The Chanticleer's resonator grille has a funky, industrial look. The designer likened it to an oil drain cover.

Collings OM2H

Michigan-born Bill Collings grew up in Ohio, but relocated to Houston, Texas in 1973. Originally, he made his living repairing guitars, but began to build his own instruments in 1975. Prominent local musicians, including Lyle Lovett, began to use Collings guitars, and his reputation grew. In 1986, Collings set up his own company.

In 1988, Collings was boosted by a significant order for 24 custom instruments from Nashville guitar dealer George Gruhn. His designs were soon attracting the attention of major names such as David Crosby, Emmylou Harris, John Prine, and even Keith Richards of the Rolling Stones. Collings currently produces eight categories of guitar.

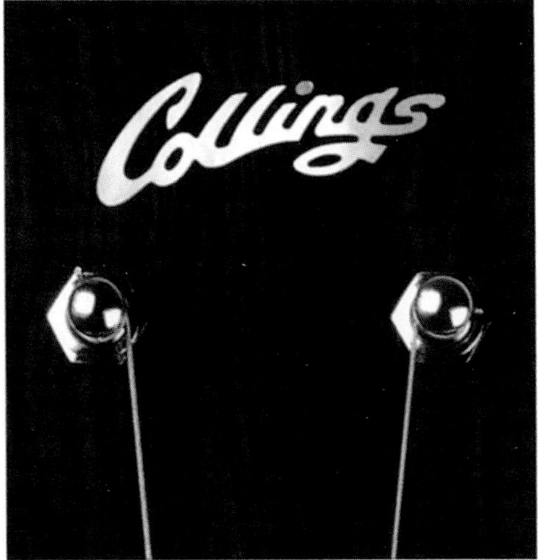

The distinctive Collings script lettering is adapted from the company's Pen and Ink drawing of its factory in Austin, Texas that appears inside the soundhole.

Coral Electric Sitar

In 1967, the short-lived Coral company introduced a curious instrument, designed by top American session guitarist Vinnie Bell in conjunctin with former Danelectro boss Nathan Daniel. This was the ''electric sitar,'' which owed its popularity to the craze for all things Indian that characterized the ''flower power'' movement. Bell's hybrid electric model featured 13 sympathetic ''drone'' strings alongside its six fretted ones.

Bell made an album Pop Goes The Electric Sitar to showcase the instrument. It remained a rare collectors' item for decades, but has recently been revived by Nathan Daniel devotee Jerry Jones. His Nashville-based company makes three versions of the sitar.

Cort SFX 6

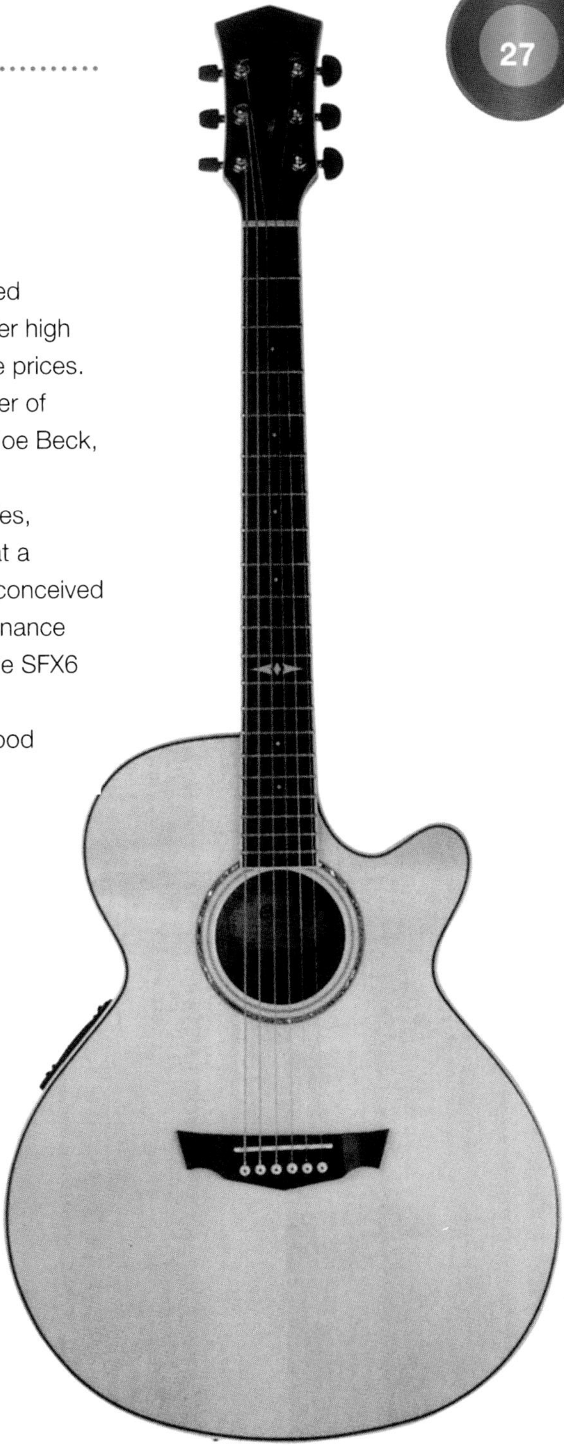

While its headquarters is in Northbrook, Illinois, Cort builds its guitars in Asia, in its own dedicated manufacturing facilities. As a result, Cort can offer high quality, U.S.-designed instruments at reasonable prices. Founded in 1960, the firm has acquired a number of high-profile endorsees, including Larry Coryell, Joe Beck, and Matt Murphy.

The company produces a range of solid-bodies, basses, acoustics, and semi-acoustics, aimed at a cross-section of players. Its SFX flat-tops were conceived as "extra light acoustics with rich tone and resonance either on the stage or [at] home unplugged." The SFX6 has a solid spruce top, mahogany neck, and rosewood back and sides.

The SFX 6's neck is mahogany; here it joins the guitar's rosewood back and sides. The chrome stud is a strap fixing.

D'Angelico Excel, 1949

John D'Angelico (1905-1964) was a New Yorker of Italian extraction. After learning his lutherie skills from his great-uncle, D'Angelico established a shop of his own in the Little Italy district of his home city in 1932. He crafted handmade archtop guitars based around four model types, Style A, Style B, Excel and New Yorker, though his also produced individual instruments customised in line with players' requirements. His output was comparatively small. Even at the peak of production in the late 1930s, D'Angelico made only around 35 instruments per year.

No more Style As or Bs appeared after 1940s, but D'Angelico continued to make his other two archtop models until his death in 1964.

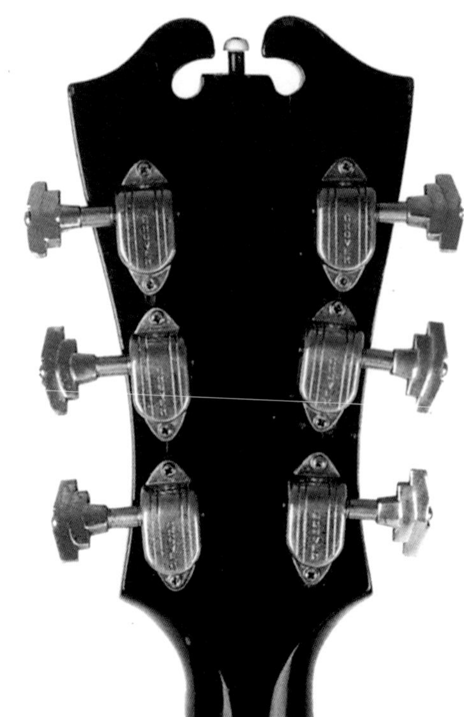

D'Angelico EXS-1DH

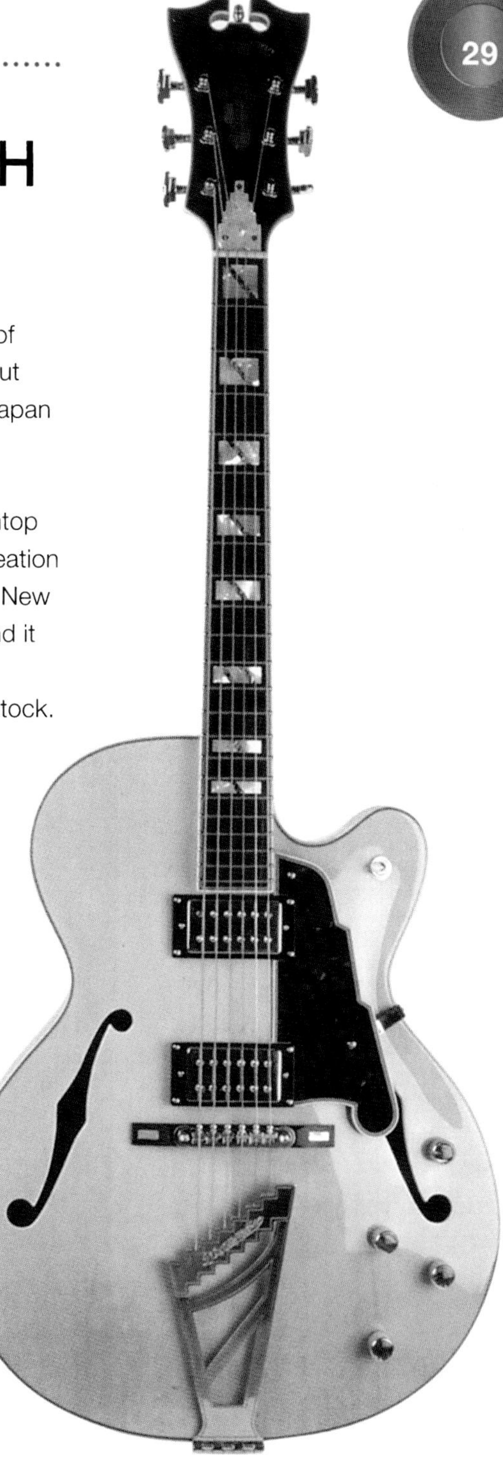

Collectors treasure original examples of John D'Angelico's lutherie. If they come onto the market, these instruments will often change hands for tens of thousands of dollars. But since 1988, high quality but affordable D'Angelico replicas have been made in Japan under the supervision of a New Jersey-based firm, D'Angelico Guitars of America.

The Excel EXS-1DH is the most inexpensive archtop in the company's current range, but is a loving recreation of John D'Angelico's design. Its name derives from New York's state motto "Excelsior" ("Ever Upward"), and it includes characteristics D'Angelico features: "split-rectangle" fret markers, and a Deco-inspired headstock.

The Excel's gold-plated hardware includes a fully adjustable bridge and two humbucking pickups made by Kent Armstrong.

D'Angelico NYL-2 (New Yorker)

The D'Angelico New Yorker featured here, like the Excel EXS-1DH is a modern replica made by D'Angelico Guitars of America. The New Yorker, which debuted in 1936, was John D'Angelico's ''top of the line'' model; and, like is own guitars, this one combines handsome looks with a ''rich and deep jazz tone.''

Its 17-inch top is an inch narrower that D'Angelico's original New Yorkers, but this and other cosmetic discrepancies do not detract from the appeal of the instrument. As John D'Angelico's health declined, he came to rely increasingly upon the skills of his last apprentice, Jimmy D'Aquisto, whom he had taken on in 1952, and with whom he had a close emotional bond.

The tailpiece is both ornate and functional.

D'Aquisto New Yorker DQ-NYE

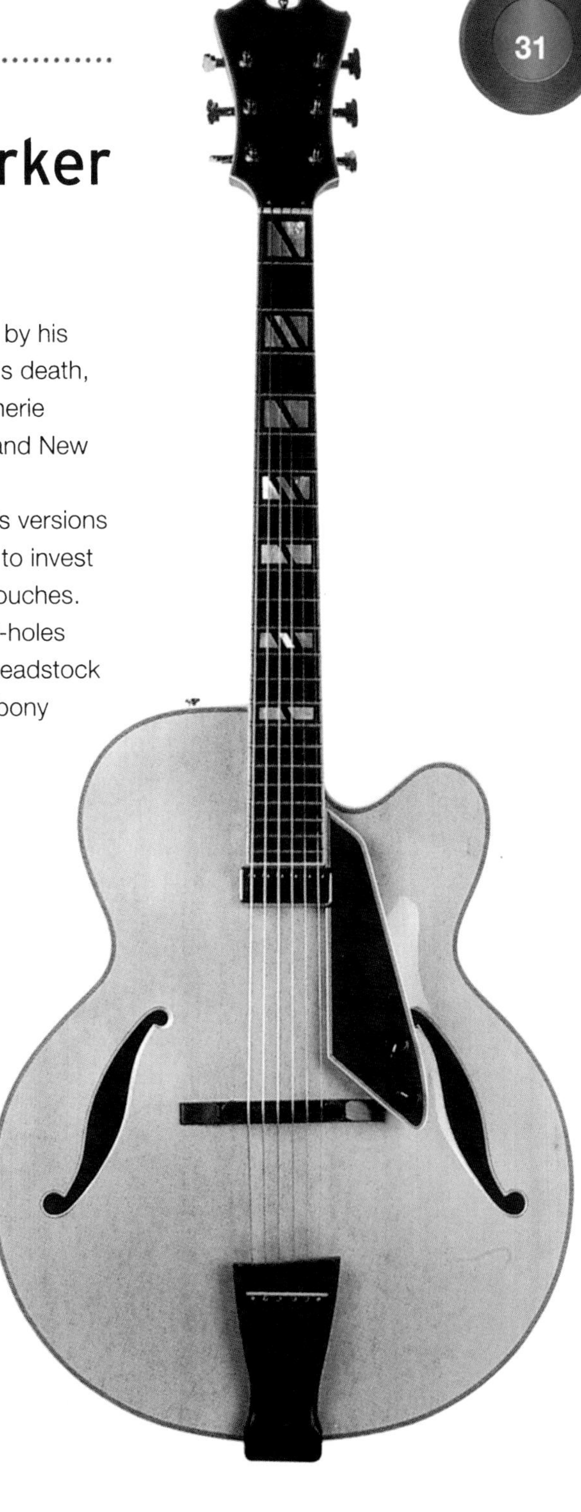

John D'Angelico's last guitars were assembled by his apprentice, Jimmy D'Aquisto. After D'Angelico's death, D'Aquisto (1935-1995) established his own lutherie business, but continued to produce the Excel and New Yorker archtop models created by his mentor.

At first, there was little difference between his versions and the originals, but in time, D'Aquisto began to invest these classic designs with his own distinctive touches. His New Yorkers gradually acquired reshaped f-holes (elliptical, with no center stroke), a scroll-type headstock in place of the "Chrysler Building" style, and ebony tailpieces.

D'Aquisto Centura DQ-CR

As well as building D'Angelico-inspired guitars, Jimmy D'Aqusito created many entirely original instruments. They seem to reflect his somewhat mixed attitude to the traditions of archtop making, which he revered, but often felt inhibited by. He told one young luthier, as Ken Vose reveals in an article published on the Museum of Musical Instruments' website, "You are so lucky. You can do anything you want; everyone expects me to build what I always build."

Despite these words, however, D'Aquisto frequently succeeded in both surprising and delighting customers and critics with his designs, before his early death at the age of only 59. This model is a replica "Centura."

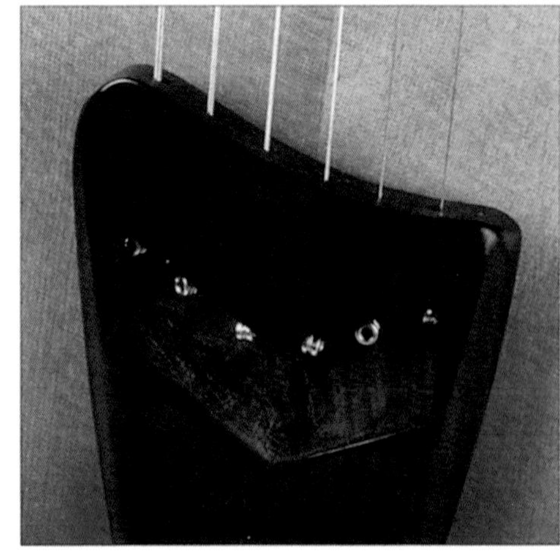

D'Aquisto's wooden tailpiece is attached to the guitar's body by a metal hinge.

Daisy Rock Pixie

Producing guitars for girls and women can be a commercially uncertain venture, but the California-based Daisy Rock company has been enjoying considerable success with a range of electrics and acoustics aimed at female players. Daisy Rock was the brainchild of Los Angeles-based Tish Ciravolo, who says that "standard guitars are often too big and bulky for the female form."

The Daisy Rock acoustic seen here is a Pixie model, finished in "Sky Blue;" "Powder Pink" and "Pixie Purple" shades are also available, and a "sister" version of the model, incorporating a piezo-electric pickup with an onboard tuner, is produced in "Plum Purple Burst" or "Blueberry Burst."

Everything about the Daisy Rock Pixie is designed to appeal to girls and young women including the dainty headstock and delicate female script of the logo.

Daisy Rock Heartbreaker Bass

The average bass guitar tends to be considerably less "woman-friendly" than its 6-string counterpart, and even iconic female bassists like Suzi Quatro complain that their favorite "axes" are very often dauntingly large and heavy.

The current range of Daisy Rock basses includes relatively conventional-looking solid, double-cutaway models such as the Elite, the Rock Candy, and the semi-hollow Retro-H. The Heartbreaker boasts a cordiform body produced in a variety of shades (this one is "Princess Purple"), and has a bolted-on, rock maple neck. The instrument weighs just under 8 pounds. It has sold well, and has become increasingly attractive to male players.

The "heart" motif extends to the markers on this model's 22-fret rosewood fingerboard.

Danelectro Solid-Body

Nathan Daniel (1912-1994) made his initial reputation as a designer and manufacturer of guitar amplifiers in the 1930s and 40s. By the mid-1950s, Daniel was also producing electric guitars at his factory in New Jersey. This model, a mid-1960s Danelectro is a typical example of Daniel's "cheap and cheerful" approach to design and construction.

Its body is made from poplar, topped and backed with stapled-on Masonite hardboard, and its single pickup is mounted inside a chrome-plated lipstick casing. Famous players, including Jimmy Page of Led Zeppelin and Tom Petty, have used Danelectros.

With a sliver of rosewood serving as a bridge saddle, little or no adjustment is possible.

Dean 'Dimebag' Tribute ML

On Wednesday December 8 2004, "Dimebag" Darrell Abbott, guitarist with the leading heavy metal band Damageplan, was gunned down on stage in Columbus, Ohio. Dimebag had formed the band with his brother, drummer Vinnie.

Among the many memorials to him was this "Tribute" guitar produced by the Dean company. The guitar shown here has an "ML"-type body, named for the late Matt Lynn. The shape was a favorite of Dimebag's, and this model is designed to resemble the early Dean models he did so much to popularize. Its features include a Floyd Rose-licensed tremolo, and a "Dimebucker" high-output pickup. The neck and body are mahogany, the fingerboard rosewood.

A picture of "Dimebag" Darrel is featured in the center of the headstock.

Dean Copper Resonator

In 1998, Dean Guitars expanded its product range, previously dominated by electric solid-bodies, to feature both acoustics and resonators. Resonators had been regarded as having only specialist appeal. Dean, however, was committed to these instruments, and launched both wood- and metal-bodied biscuit-bridge types, as well as a spider-bridge, Dobro-like model, the "SP." In 2004, Dean introduced two new "Heirloom" resonators. Like their predecessors, they are popular among blues players with limited funds, but have also been praised by leading players such as blues picker and bandleader Patrick Sweany. These models are both single-cones. This instrument is in "distressed copper."

Dobro (1)

In early 1929, John Dopyera (1893-1988) resigned from the board of the Los Angeles-based National company. His departure followed a dispute over the ownership of the design for a single-cone resonator that he and his brother Rudy had developed for National.

Together with their other siblings Emil, Robert, and Louis, they now formed a rival resonator guitar-making firm called Dobro. "Dobro" is both an abbreviation of "Dopyera Brothers," and the Slovakian for "good." John and Rudy Dopyera now invented an alternative resonator. Rudy filed a patent application for it in June 1929. But some experts maintain that Dobro instruments were already using the design.

The guitar's headstock facing is rosewood with inset mother of pearl lettering.

Dobro (2)

The new Dobro resonator was dish shaped, and made from aluminum. Its bridge, nicknamed a "spider" is also metal, and had a central section (with a wooden saddle on top of it) making contact with the strings. It also has eight radiating "legs" that carry vibrations to the edge of the cone.

The resonator's excellent design means that its sound has more resonance and longer sustain than the National version. When demand outpaced supply in 1932, the brothers signed a licensing agreement with Chicago manufacturer, Regal. In 1935, resolving their dispute with National, the companies merged, forming National-Dobro. The model shown is later copy of metal Model 36.

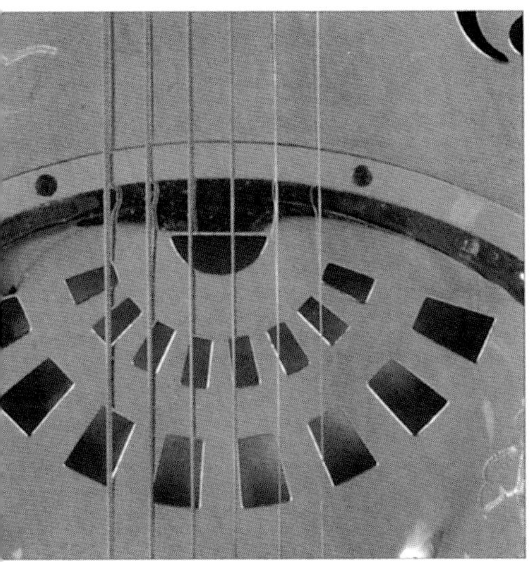

"Fan"-style coverplate holes such as these occur on many Dobro instruments

Patrick Eggle New York

British-born guitar maker Patrick Eggle first became involved with lutherie as a schoolboy. In 1991, businessman Andrew Selby set up Patrick Eggle Guitars to manufacture his designs. The company was located in the English city of Coventry. Amongst its early successes were the Berlin and New York models. This New York is finished in "Fire Engine Red."

By the mid-1990s, Eggle was producing up to 2,000 guitars a year, but Patrick Eggle himself left the company in 1995. He returned to smaller scale, "heirloom" guitar production, concentrating on building flat-top and archtop acoustic guitars. Now trading as Patrick James Eggle, Eggle has relocated to North Carolina.

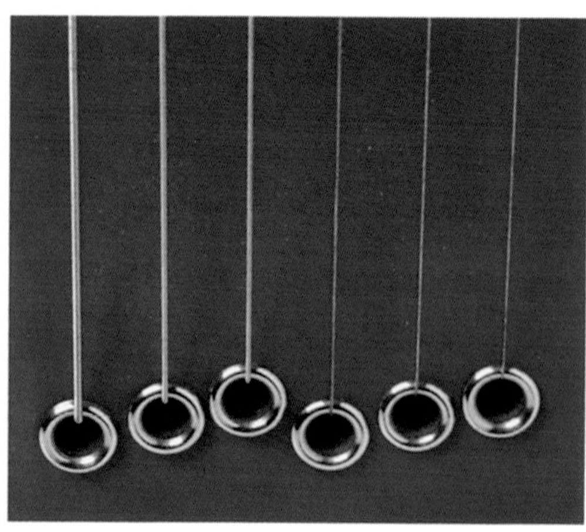

The New York has chrome-steel grommet inlets to secure the strings at the tail end.

Epiphone Masterbilt

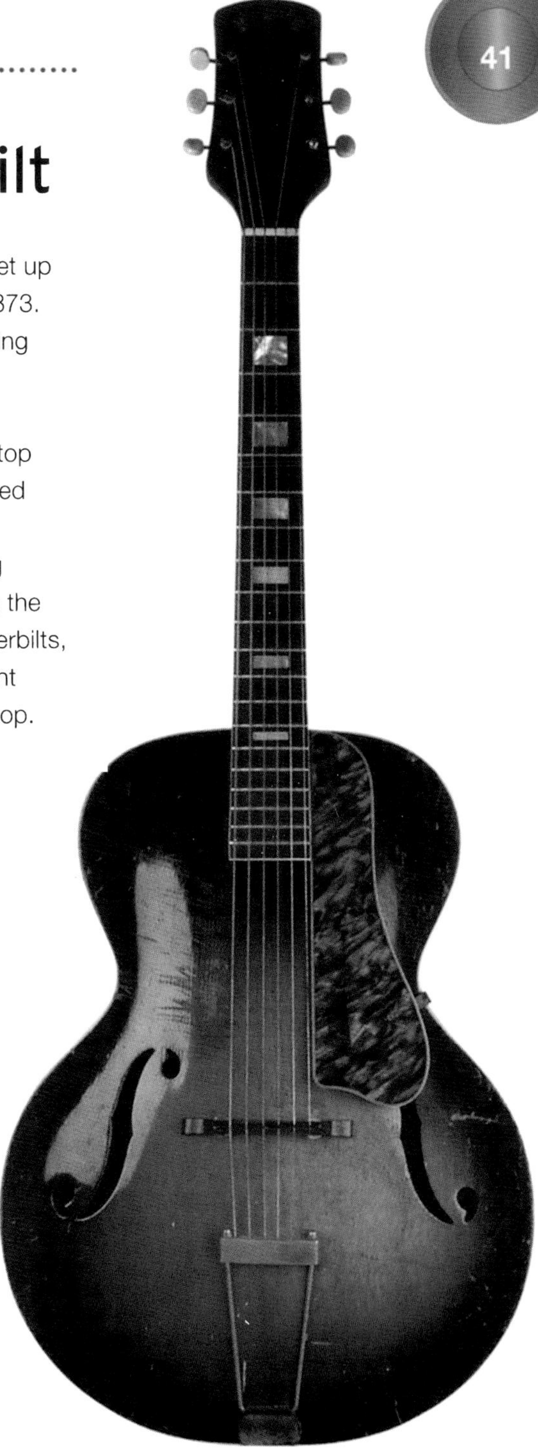

The New-York based House of Stathopoulo was set up by Greek immigrant, Anastasios Stathopoulo, in 1873. The company switched from violin making to building fretted instruments under the management of Anastasios's son Epaminondas (''Epi''). Renamed ''Epiphone,'' the company introduced its first archtop acoustic guitars in the 1920s. Its factory was located in New York's Long Island City.

Within a decade, Epiphone guitars were rivalling Gibsons in terms of both sales and quality. Among the company's most successful models were its Masterbilts, launched in 1931. This sunburst-finished instrument dates from around this time. It has a solid spruce top.

The Epiphone declares its US roots proudly; the factory was located in Long Island, New York.

Epiphone Granada

The death of Epiphone's founder, Epi Stathopoulo, in 1943 ushered in difficult times for the company, and its market share declined. Meanwhile, Epiphone's principal rival, Gibson, had appointed a dynamic new president, Ted McCarty, in 1948. Gibson's profits increased, and their manufacturing capacity expanded. In 1957, McCarty advised Gibson's owners, Chicago Musical Instruments (CMI) to purchase Epiphone at the bargain price of $20,000. Epiphone subsequently relocated to Gibson's headquarters in Kalamazoo, Michigan, and an increasing number of Epiphones became cheaper, slightly modified versions of existing Gibson designs. Launched in 1962, the Granada bears a striking resemblance to Gibson's thinline body ES-120T.

Epiphone's distinctive company logo is based on the Greek letter epsilon.

Epiphone Casino

Like the Granada, the Epiphone Casino, introduced in 1961, is a close copy of an existing Gibson model, in this case the 1959 ES-330. Both guitars resembled the Gibson ES-335, although the 330 and Casino were true hollow-bodies, lacking the 335's center block. They were also fitted with single-coil, P-90 pickups. The distinctive "dog-ear" pickup covers on the first Casinos were black, with "dot" fret markers and mock-tortoiseshell pickguards.

These features all changed within a few years. This Casino, dating from 1964, has a white pickguard, nickel-covered P-90s, and "parallelogram" neck inlays. The Casino is described as "the guitar that put Epiphone on the map."

White pickguards with the Epsilon logo first appeared on the Casino in 1963.

Epiphone Casino (John Lennon 1965)

The Epiphone Casino sold well in the USA, and subsequently attracted the attention of some high-profile overseas customers: The Beatles. It was actually Paul McCartney who first used one during a Beatles recording session in London in 1965. The following year, however, George Harrison and John Lennon purchased their own Casinos, and while Harrison did not play his very frequently, Lennon almost immediately adopted the Epiphone as his principal electric guitar, and continued to feature Casinos on live gigs and recordings for the rest of his life. Gibson celebrated John Lennon's links with the instrument by producing limited edition replicas in both 1999 and 2005.

Epiphone Sorrento

Gibson's ES-125T, a thinline electric with a single P-90 pickup, was introduced in 1956. It had been conceived as a relatively low-priced addition to the company's range, but an even less costly alternative model was provided four years later: the Epiphone Sorrento. Like other Epis of the period, it closely replicated its Gibson original and was manufactured alongside it in Kalamazoo, Michigan. Both the ES-125T and Sorrento had bodies constructed from maple plywood, and a single, sharp-horned cutaway. This example is from 1967. Sorrento fans include Noel Gallagher of Oasis, who recently auctioned one of his instruments for a substantial sum.

Despite the distinctive Epiphone logo, the Sorrento is essentially a slightly modified Gibson design.

Epiphone Olympic

The original Epiphone Olympic was an acoustic archtop from pre-war days. Almost a decade after its discontinuation, its name was given to a solid-body electric that debuted in 1960. The new Olympic was almost identical to the Melody Maker electric then being produced by Epi's owners, Gibson. Both instruments had single-cutaways, "3-a-side" headstocks, and pickups built into their pickguards.

The next stage in the evolution of the Olympic was in 1962, when the Olympic Special joined the single-cutaway model. An asymmetrical body replaced the original styling in 1963. A Greek "epsilon" symbol adorned the pickguard. Both Olympics went out of production in 1970.

The tailpiece shows signs that the vibrato fitted to this mid-1960s model as standard has been removed.

Epiphone Frontier

Epiphone launched an extensive range of new instruments in 1942. Among them were several acoustic, dreadnought-styled models. One of the most popular of thee guitars proved to be the FT-110, the immediate ancestor of the Epiphone Frontier seen here. The FT-30 (''Caballero''), and FT-79 (''Texan'') models debuted at the same time. In its original form, the FT-110 was round-shouldered, and had a comparatively plain finish. Like other Epiphone flat-tops, it acquired a squarer shape when Gibson took over the company in 1957. In 1964, the guitar acquired its distinctive ''cactus-and-rope''-decorated pickguard. Promotional material described its sound as being ''authentically American.'' The Frontier was discontinued in 1970. This example is from 1964.

The inlays on this 1964 Frontier's pickguard are still in almost pristine condition.

Epiphone Joe Perry Les Paul

Gibson's takeover by Norlin Industries in 1969 led to big changes at Epiphone. Within a year, Epi manufacturing had been switched to the Far East, and it became no more than a conduit for cheap copies of Gibson models. Recently, however, Epiphone has regained a character of its own. The Joe Perry Les Paul model was launched in 2004. A Gibson Signature Model endorsed by the Aerosmith star inspired it, and shares the "Aged Tiger" finish of the original.

This finish was created by Perry's wife Billie, first seen on a Gibson Custom Shop axe she gave him as a birthday gift. Its pickups, like those on the Signature Les Paul, are USA-made Burstbuster II and IIIs.

Ivory colored plastic mountings for the guitar's selector switch contrast nicely with the "Aged Tiger' yellow stained maple.

Epiphone Bob Marley Les Paul

In 2002, Gibson saluted the late Bob Marley with a limited edition model based on his Les Paul Special. A year later, Epiphone launched its own Marley guitar. The instrument's mahogany body is overlaid with a picture of Marley's face, while the rectangular position markers on its fingerboard are red, gold, and green; widely regarded as Jamaica's national colors.

The headstock carries the words "One Love," the title of the classic Marley song featured on his 1977 Exodus LP, and there is a mocked-up "signature" on its truss-rod cover. Like its more expensive Gibson counterpart, the Epiphone Marley Commemorative Les Paul has a deliberately "worn-in" brown finish.

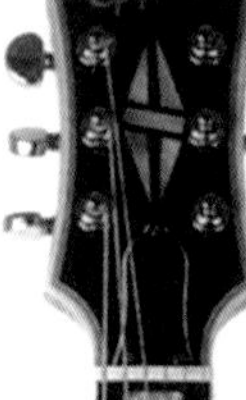

Epiphone Zakk Wylde 'Buzzsaw'

Guitarist Zakk Wylde first came to prominence in the late 1980s as part of hard rock legend Ozzy Osbourne's group, and has gone on to massive success with the band Black Label Society. Epiphone currently produces three Les Paul Specials carrying his name: all have similar specifications, but boast different, equally flamboyant finishes.

The "Buzzsaw" model is based on one of Zakk Wylde's own instruments: the design on its top was inspired by a pattern on a cigarette lighter belonging to Tim Bolin, Black Label Society's tour manager. The background color was chosen to match the "General Lee" automobile featured in Zakk's favorite TV show, The Dukes of Hazzard.

A distinctive logo depicting Zakk Wylde sporting obligatory flares appears on the headstock.

Epiphone Dot Studio

The Epiphone DOT, launched in 1996, was closely based on the classic Gibson ES-335 "semi-hollow" electric. The Dot Studio, while retaining the shape and basic attributes of its predecessor, is simpler and more streamlined.

Its two pickups have no individual volume and tone controls, and the traditional 335-style pickguard and fretboard position markers (the "dots" for which the model was named) have vanished, while the sunburst, cherry, and natural finishes provided for the older DOT have been replaced with a choice of striking new colors. These include "Lemon" (as seen here), "Tomato," "Ice Blue," and "Dolphin Gray." This model has Alnico-V humbucker pickups.

Black (instead of chrome) is an unusual but effective color coordination choice for this model.

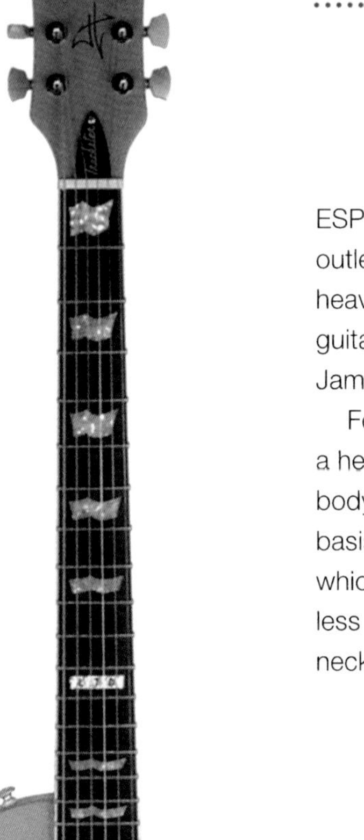

EPS LTD Truckster

ESP (''Electric Sound Products'') began in 1975 as a retail outlet in Tokyo. As the company's fame spread, among the heavy metal fraternity, it switched to full-time production of guitars and basses. In 1991, Megadeath founder member James Hetfield began using ESP instruments.

For the group's 2003/4 ''St. Anger'' tour, ESP built him a heavily modified version of its successful Truckster solid-body. Its specification and appearance were used as the basis for ESP's Hetfield ''Signature Model'' Truckster, which debuted in 2005. The ''axe'' is available from ESP's less expensive LTD range. It has a mahogany body and neck, EMG pickups, and a rosewood fingerboard.

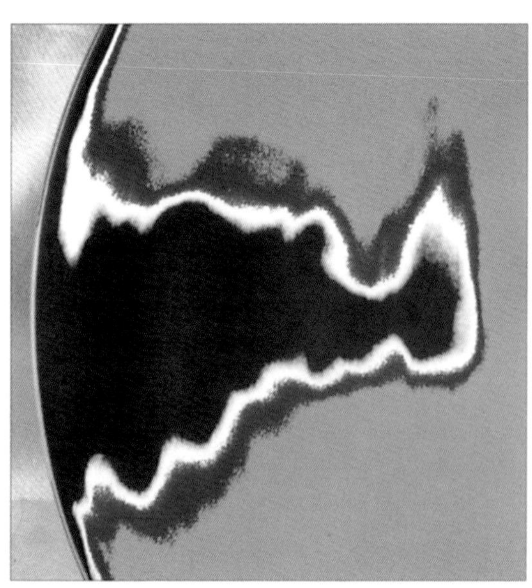

A simulated blemish made by rubbing the finish back to the basecoat replicates the one on James Hetfield's own ''axe.''

Fender 'No-Caster' Replica

Leo Fender (1909-1991) was fascinated by electronics since boyhood, and after a brief stint working as an accountant, he set up a radio repair shop in Fullerton, California. Fender went on to produce guitars and amplifiers in collaboration with local musician Clayton O. ("Doc") Kauffman, under the K&F brand name. When this partnership ended in 1946, Leo founded the Fender Electric Instrument Company.

In 1950, he introduced a solid-bodied electric guitar for "Spanish-style" playing, with a wooden slab body and bolted-on neck. Originally named the Esquire, Fender re-named it the Broadcaster, and finally the "No-caster" after a trademark dispute with Gretsch.

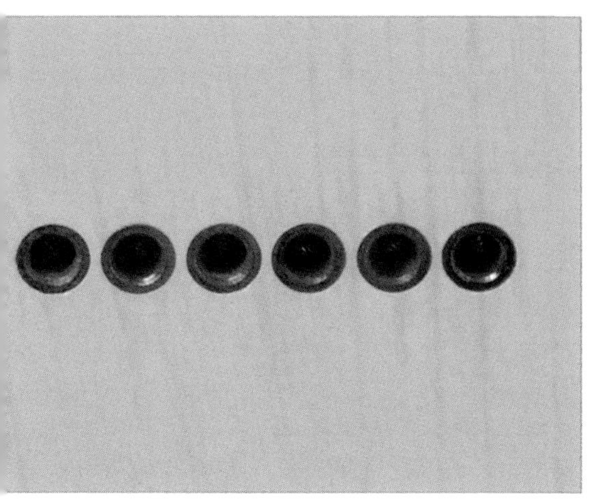

This method of fastening strings inside the Fender guitar's body is both neat and secure.

Fender 1952 Telecaster Replica

Gretsch manufactured Broadkaster drumkits and forced Fender to abandon this model name for his innovative guitar. It is said that Don Randall, Fender's distributor, came up with the name of Telecaster. Its Spartan simplicity of design evoked a mixed response, but it was also immensely practical. It was also reasonably priced at $190. Fender continued to refine its design and features over the years.

The electrics became much simpler, and simpler switching was substituted. Black bakelite pickguards were replaced with white ones in 1954. Genuine 1952 Telecasters sell for very large sums, but skilfully aged replicas like this one are much more affordable.

A plain wooden (ash) body and black pickguard are hallmarks of pre-1964 Fenders. Later models had painted finishes and the more familiar white pickguards.

Fender Precision Bass

The stand-up double bass, played pizzicato, was a standard fixture in many popular music combos for the first half of the twentieth century. But the instrument had three major drawbacks. It was too quiet, and often could not be heard over louder instruments; it was very large and unwieldy; and difficult to keep in tune. Fender managed to solve all three problems with his precision bass guitar, launched in 1951.

Its slim, solid body was smaller and lighter than its "stand-up" rivals; its single pickup supplied a clear, sustained sound; while its fretted neck helped accurate intonation. Rival companies soon started to design their own electric basses to compete.

The distinctive Fender logo has worn off slightly, part of the aging process marking the guitar's fifty years of useful life.

Fender Stratocaster ('Relic')

Fender's revolutionary Stratocaster debuted in 1954, and it quickly took the guitar world by storm. Unlike the Telecaster, the Stratocaster had a vibrato mechanism controlled by a pivoting bridge section, three pickups, a double cutaway, and a contoured body design. Its ergonomic feel was particularly popular. The instrument originally sold for $249.50, but original models are now worth very large sums of money.

Many aspire instead to deliberately aged "Relic" models produced by the Fender Custom Shop in 1995. This is a replica of Mary Kaye's 1956 "custom-color" Strat, complete with gold fittings. Singer and guitarist Kaye was a major star of the 50s and 60s.

The back of guitar shows deliberate wear and carefully aged screws to create the "relic" look from a modern guitar.

Fender Mark Knopfler Stratocaster

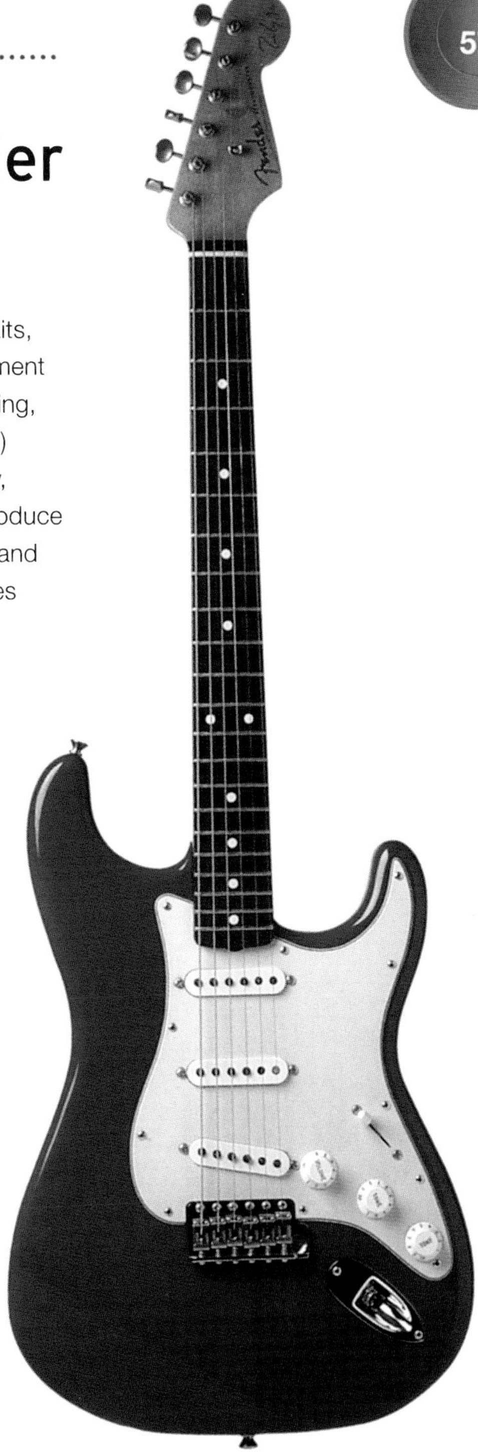

One famous Fender user, Mark Knopfler of Dire Straits, owns a 1961 ''Fiesta Red'' Stratocaster. The instrument is featured on many of his classic recordings (including, most famously, the 1978/79 hit ''Sultans of Swing.'') Knopfler also continues to use the guitar extensively, both onstage and in the studio. Fender began to produce replicas of Knopfler's guitar in 2003, whose woods and colors exactly replicate the 1960s original, but carries Mark Knopfler's autograph on the headstock.

The model is part of Fender's ''Artist Signature Series.'' Unlike the earlier models, the guitar has a 5-way pickup selector. The original pickup switch was a 3-way device. This was replaced in 1977.

The controls on the pickguard showing the 5-way selector pickup switch which allowed the player to activate all the pickups simultaneously.

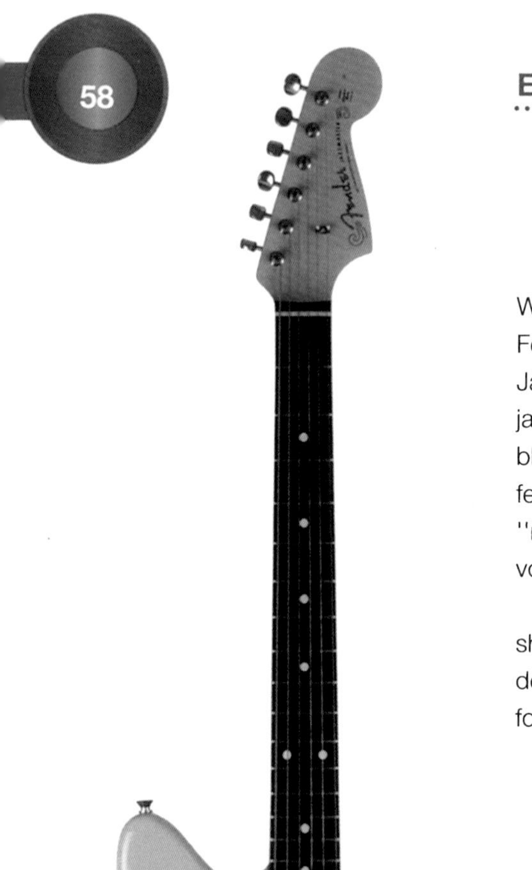

Fender Jazzmaster

Within a few years of launching the Stratocaster, Leo Fender was working on a major new electric guitar, the Jazzmaster. As its name suggested, this was aimed at the jazz fraternity rather than the rockers, country pickers, and bluesmen that had favored the Telecaster and Strat. It featured mellower sounding pickups, plus a switchable "rhythm circuit" for the neck transducer, allowing its volume and tone to be present for playing backing chords.

There was also a locking vibrato, and a body that was shaped to maximize comfort for seated players. The guitar debuted in 1958 and it attracted a good deal of criticism for its unstable bridge, excessive weight, and odd shape.

Fender Custom Telecaster

Launched in 1959, the Custom Telecaster was the first Fender production-model Tele to have a binding around its body. (Three Telecasters, and a Precision Bass had been made with bindings in 1958 as custom made instruments for country music star Buck Owens and his band members Don Rich and Doyle Holly.) The new Telecaster had some other distinctive features. Its neck, for example, instead of being all-maple as on previous Fenders, was a two-piece component made from alder with a rosewood fingerboard.

The traditional blonde finish and black pickguard were also replaced, with a sunburst paint job and white pickguard. This example dates from 1965. It has a crude bridge with shared saddles.

A close up of the relatively crude bridge, with shared saddles used on previous Telecasters.

Fender Jazz Bass

Introduced in 1960, the Jazz Bass represented a considerable advance on Fender's previous Precision model. Most immediately noticeable was its reshaped, "off-set" body; there were also two pickups, built-in mutes for each string, and a narrower neck that permitted nimbler fingerwork.

Early Jazz Basses featured two "stacked" knobs (one for each pickup), which combined volume and tone controls on a single shaft. The mutes were dropped some three years later. A revamped instrument was introduced in 1989. This had 22 frets (two more than on the original version). This is the model shown here. Perhaps the most famous Jazz Bass user was Jaco Pastorius of Weather Report.

Fender Jaguar

Fender announced the Jaguar in 1962. It had a number of novel features, including a neck with a 24-inch scale (1 1/2 inches shorter than a Telecaster or Stratocaster) and was designed to appeal to musicians with smaller hands. A string mute was installed between the back pickup and the bridge.

This could be "activated or disengaged by the light touch of a finger." It was possible to combine either or both of the Jaguar's pickups, while a separate set of controls allowed players to pre-set volume and tone levels for rhythm. It also had a "Synchronized tremolo." The instrument was discontinued in 1974, but developed a cult following. This is a modern example, made in Japan.

Two of these three switches control the Jaguar's pickups: the third engages the guitar's bass-cut (a.k.a. "strangle") circuitry.

Fender Mustang

Although professionals and serious amateurs were Fender's best customers, Leo retained an interest in the lucrative beginners' market. In 1956, Fender produced its first "Spanish" (i.e. non lap-steel student guitars, the rather plain and unsophisticated Musicmaster and Duo-Sonic.

The firm decided to revamp its existing student models in the 1960s and introduced the Mustang in 1964. It resembled the Duo-Sonic, but also had "dynamic vibrato." Fender patented this feature. Its presence was a key selling point for the guitar, as were its red, white, and blue "patriotic colors." The little guitar was discontinued in 1982. This is a later Japanese-made example.

Fender Mustang Bass

Fender's Mustang Bass was introduced in 1966. A beginner's model with a single, split-coil pickup, its chief selling point was its 30-scale. This made the Mustang "ideal for the student and musician with short reach." The bass was initially offered in the same red, white, and blue colors as the Mustang guitar.

Despite its modest status, the Mustang bass has attracted a surprising number of high profile players, including Tina Weymouth of Talking Heads, and Bill Wyman of the Rolling Stones. Fender's decision to start producing the model again in 2002 was warmly welcomed by many players, both amateur and professional. Fender built this 2005 Mustang in Japan.

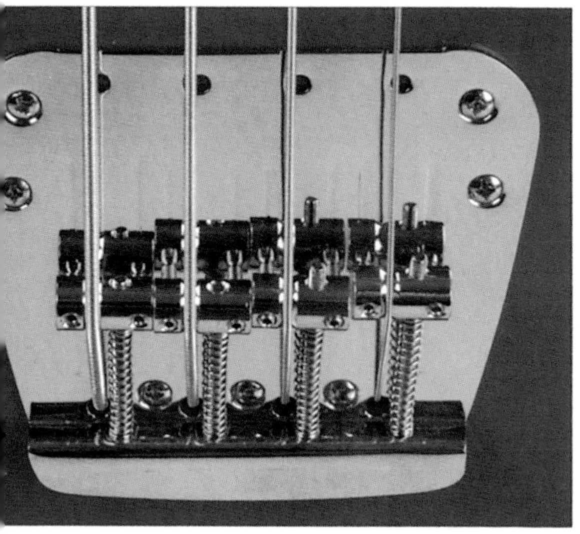

The tailpiece on the Fender Mustang Bass is an extremely robust and well-engineered feature of its construction.

Fender 'Floral' Telecaster (Japan)

In the wake of the 1967 "Summer of Love," Fender made the slightly surprising decision to produce Telecasters and Telecaster basses decorated in hippy-influenced "blue floral" and "pink paisley." They first appeared in 1968.

The paisley model achieved considerable prominence when James Burton, the lead guitarist for Elvis Presley, began to use the instrument on live shows and TV appearances with "The King." But these unusually finished teles did not sell well, and they were discontinued in 1969. Nostalgia for 60s style resulted in a reissue in the mid-1980s by Fender's Japanese division. Discontinued once more, the models were reintroduced in 2002/3.

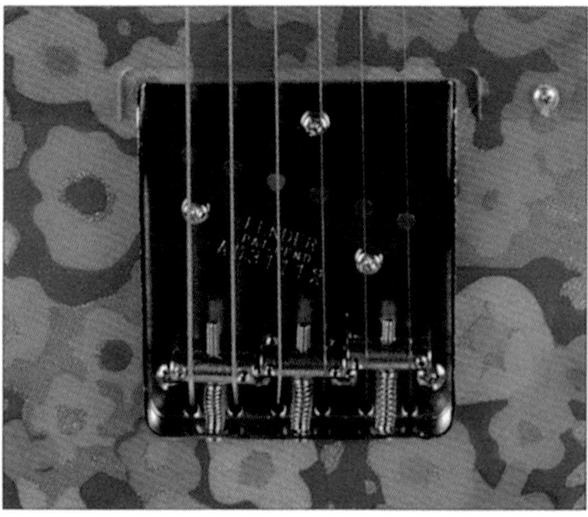

The hippy-influenced blue floral pattern is in stark contrast with the Fender tail end no-nonsense hardware and patent stamp.

Fender Electric XII

By the mid-1960s, the rich jangling timbre of the 12-string guitar was the sound of the moment, and Leo Fender hoped that his Electric XII solid-body, introduced in 1965, would challenge more established 12-string manufacturers, such as Rickenbacker. The new guitar had a strikingly shaped headstock, and a pair of pickups with split groups of pole-pieces to enrich the tone of the lower strings and add edge and clarity to their treble counterparts.

It also boasted an ingeniously designed bridge, which made the guitar easier to finger. The guitar attracted several leading players, including The Who's Peter Townsend, and Jimmy Page of Led Zeppelin (on "Stairway to Heaven," 1971).

The guitar's pickups can be used singly or together, and there is a deep tone setting that can be switched into circuit by the selector knob.

Fender Coronado II Antigua

In January 1965, Columbia Broadcasting System (CBS) purchased Fender for just over $13,000,000. The change of ownership was precipitated by Leo's poor health and the need to fund expansion of the business. New management introduced new products. The most striking of these were the Coronados, Fender's first-ever non-solid body electrics. Roger Rossmeisl, who had previously worked for Rickenbacker, designed the Coronado I and II (with one and two pickups respectively), and a 12-stringer.

They were launched in 1966, and were available in both regular and stained-beech "Wildwood" versions. "Antigua" (a curious black-brown-silver shading) came out in 1968.

Antigua coloring was later applied to several Fender solids, including Telecasters and Stratocasters.

Fender Fretless Precision Bass

Fretless basses were rarities during the mid-to-late 1960s: the highest profile model then in circulation was Ampeg's AUB-1, introduced, along with its fretted cousin, the AEB-1, in 1966. Ampeg aimed the AUB-1 primarily at stand-up players who wanted to make the transition to bass guitar, but it was also adopted by a handful of rock performers, including Rick Danko of The Band. Though still small, the fretless market was one that Fender soon decided to involve itself in, and it introduced a fretless option on its classic Precision bass in 1970.

Shown in an example from the mid-70s, the guitar received a boost in 1972 when John Paul Jones of Led Zeppelin used one onstage.

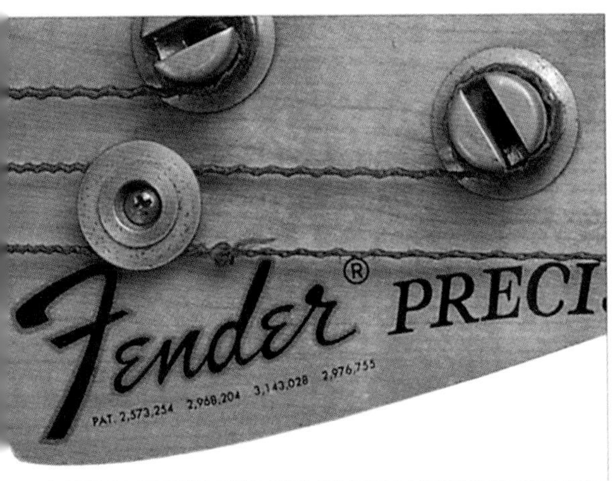

A 1970s Fender catalog described the Precision as "the most well-known and widely used electric bass in the world."

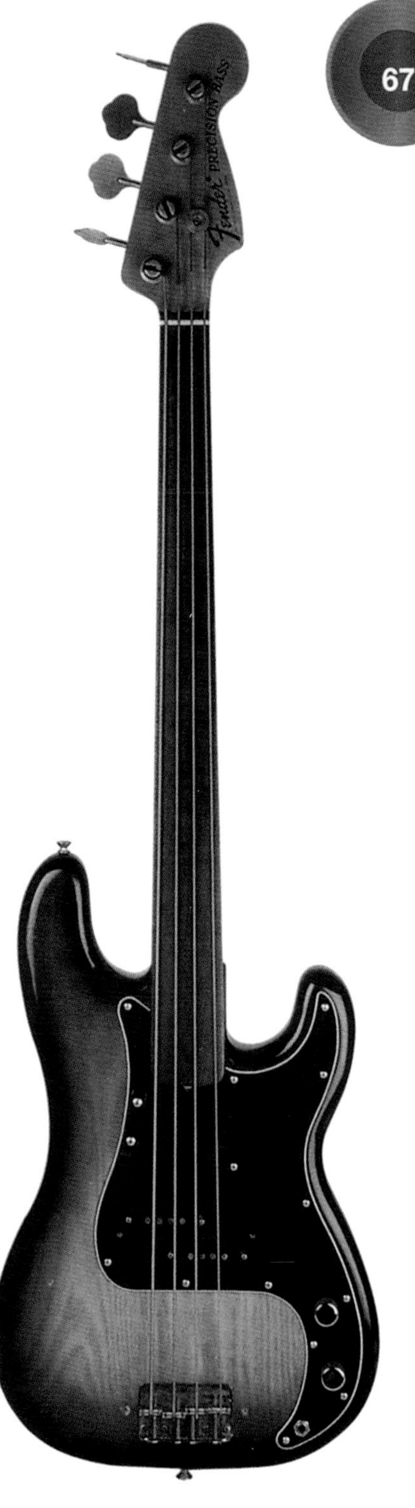

Fender Telecaster Thinline

In the mid-to-late 1960s, Fender and its CBS masters were hungry for novelty, and the increased profits that it could bring. The company began experimenting with one of its staple products, the Telecaster.

Some players had found the Tele too heavy, and in 1968, an attempt was made to solve this problem by routing out substantial sections of the body, adding an f-hole, and marketing the result as the Telecaster Thinline. Offered in a choice of "natural" finishes (mahogany or ash), the adapted Tele underwent further modification in 1972, when its single-coil pickups were replaced with humbuckers designed by former Gibson staffer Seth Lover, as shown on this 1972 example.

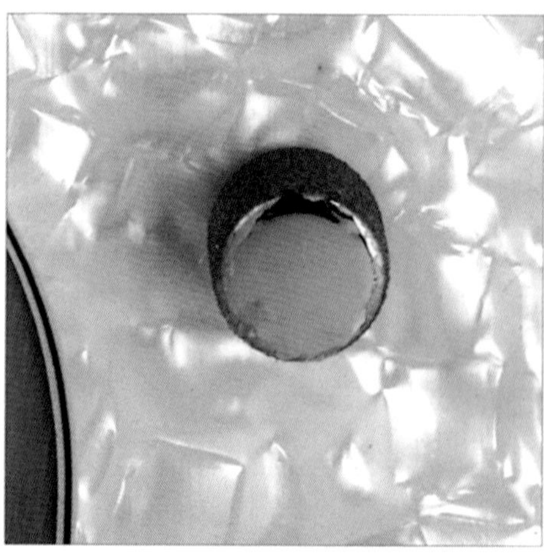

The classic Fender pickup controls look rather different when surrounded by a glossy, marbled finish pickguard.

Fender Telecaster Deluxe

The Seth Lover "wide range" humbucking pickups installed on the Thinline Telecaster reappeared on two other early-70s Teles: a new version of the Custom, fitted with a neck-position humbucker; and the Deluxe, which boasted twin double-coil units, and debuted in 1972. Like the revamped Custom, the Deluxe had individual volume and tone knobs for its transducers, with a small pickup selector on its upper bass bout replacing the chunky, but eminently practical "lever-switch" designed by Leo Fender. It had an all-maple neck and fingerboard, and chrome-plated hardware. The Deluxe was discontinued in 1981, but made a comeback in January 2004. This is a recent example.

Bridge, pickup covers and other hardware on this instrument are chrome plated.

Fender Telecaster, 1976

Among connoisseurs of vintage guitars, Fenders made before 1965 are widely regarded as superior to those produced during the CBS period (1965-1985). This judgement fails to recognize many guitars of this era, including this 1976 Telecaster. With its elegant sunburst finish, fast neck, and gutsy tone, is an excellent, highly collectible model.

In 1981, CBS brought in a new management team that included Bill Schultz. Schultz became the president of Fender and headed the group that bought out CBS in 1985 (for $12.5 million). Schultz went on to serve as Fender CEO for the next two decades, and the company prospered and expanded during this time.

The Fender "F" was registered as a trademark in 1967,but first used several years earlier.

Fender Bullet

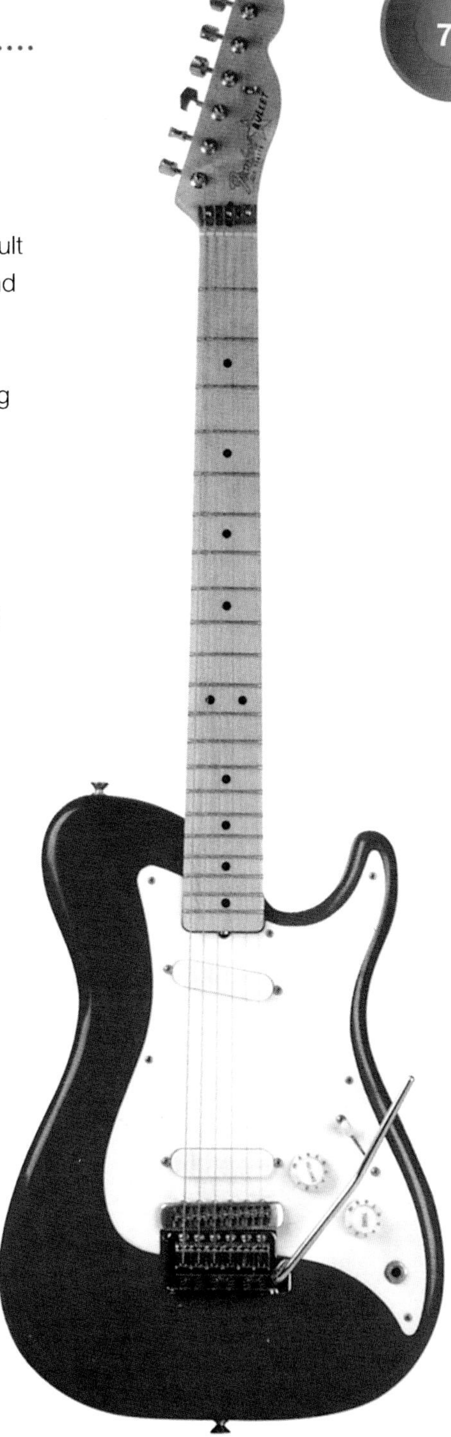

Though the CBS years are generally regarded as difficult ones for Fender, the company continued to employ and train some outstanding craftsmen. Among them was John Page, who began his career at the firm in 1978. In the early 1980s, he was given the task of developing a replacement "student" guitar for the Mustang. His design needed to be inspiring for beginners, robust, and cost-effective.

By this time, Fender was under threat from the growing number of cheap Far Eastern imports. Page responded by creating the Bullet, a two-pickup model with a Telecaster-style neck and a Stratocaster-like body. It sold for $189, and debuted in 1981. Page finally left Fender in 1998.

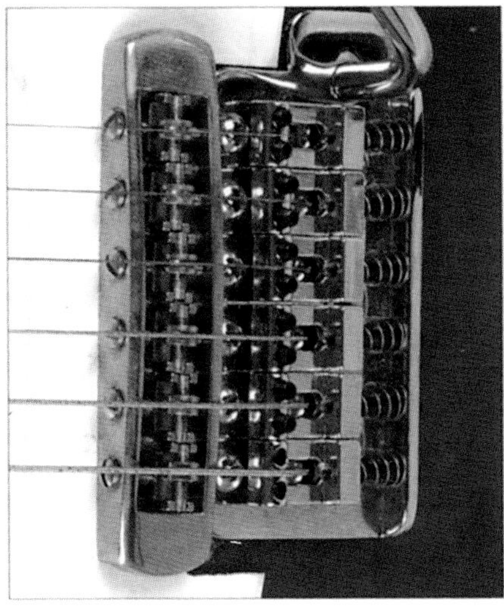

According to available records, the very first Bullets did not have vibratos; the unit seen above is probably a later addition.

Fender Custom Shop HLE

Homer Haynes and Jethro Burns were an immensely successful duo whose act combined comedy and country music. Their career began in the 1930s, and many of their best-selling records were parodies of classic popular songs. Jethro played mandolin, while Homer was a guitarist who favored Fender Stratocasters.

David Gilmour of Pink Floyd now owns one of his former guitars. In the late 1950s, Homer Haynes began using a custom 1957 Strat with an all-gold finish; three decades later, it was decided that the Fender Custom Shop (set up in 1987) should issue 300 replicas of it. The ensuing HLE (Haynes Limited Edition) was later increased to a run of 500 guitars.

This close-up shows the model's individual number and the Fender Custom Shop logo.

Fender Custom Clapton Strat

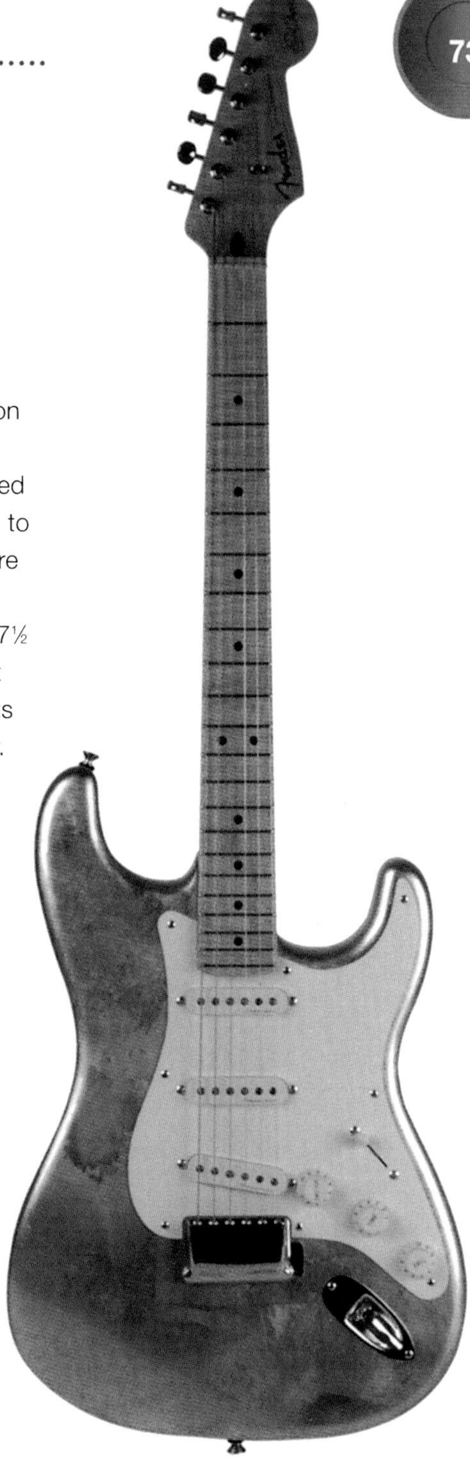

Chris Fleming is a Senior Master Building at Fender's Custom Shop: this example of his work is one of a limited edition run of ten gold leaf covered Eric Clapton Signature Stratocasters made in 2003. It closely resembles the EC-1 guitar that Clapton himself ordered from the Custom Shop in the mid-1990s; he went on to use EC-1 extensively in the studio and onstage, before auctioning it in 2004 for over $400,000.

This Custom Shop-built guitar's body weighs just 7½ pounds, and, as is customary on Fender Master Built guitars, carries its maker's signature on the back of its neck heel and also boasts a certificate of authenticity. Models like these are highly collectible.

Custom Shop models such as this with Eric Clapton's signature on the headstock are highly collectible.

Fender 'Tele 52'

Over half a century since its first appearance, the Fender Telecaster remains a favorite with players at every level. It is currently available in a bewildering number of versions. Fender's second great guitar, the Stratocaster, was meant to "obsolesce the Telecaster." This prospect was unlikely then, and is unthinkable now. Different performers may express a preference for the more sophisticated Strat or the raw, basic Tele, but each deserves to be celebrated for its own distinctive qualities.

The "Tele 52" in our pictures is a modern homage to the early days of the guitar. Although the black finish is anachronistic (black Teles did not appear until later), it is both elegant and functional.

The pickup controls and other hardware on the Tele 52 are shaped and positioned like their 1950s counterparts.

Fender Showmaster

The Telecaster and Stratocaster are classics, but Fender is keen to expand it range by developing exciting new electric guitars. Launched in 1998 as a Custom Shop model, the Fender Showmaster's neck was "set" (glued in), rather than bolted on.

Hot pickups and attractive styling won the Showmaster many admirers, and it was soon being mass-produced in a variety of versions. This example was made in the Far East, and features a flame maple top over a basswood body (quilted maple and bubinga are also available), Seymour Duncan pickups and a 24-fret fretboard. Striking a careful balance between novelty and tradition, the Showmaster seems destined for even wider popularity.

A two-point synchronized vibrato is fitted to the guitar; its arm has been removed for our photographs.

Fender Toronado

The town of Ensenada lies some 70 miles down the Pacific Coast from Tijuana, in Mexico's Baja California region. Fender opened a small packaging plant there in 1987, but within a few years, the factory was producing mid-priced versions of classic Fender designs. In 1998, the Toronado was the first-ever Mexican designed and built Fender.

It was a solid-body electric with an offset waist and two humbucking pickups. Four different finishes were available (''Arctic White,'' ''Black,'' ''Brown Sunburst,'' and ''Candy Apple Red''). An American version of the instrument was introduced in 2002. Two other colors were introduced, ''Butterscotch Blond'' and ''Crimson Transparent.''

The ''Butterscotch Blond'' paint finish here contrasts very effectively with the black selector switch surround.

Fender 'Sting' Precision Bass

Guitars owned or signed by famous musicians can change hands for vast amounts of money. Instruments in this select category are almost invariably Fenders. "Blackie," the Stratocaster used regularly by Eric Clapton on gigs and recordings for the best part of two decades, raised $959,000 for charity when auctioned by Christie's in New York.

This guitar is a Mexican-made Precision bass that British bassist, singer, and songwriter Sting (Gordon Sumner) used only once, on a BBC radio broadcast in 1994. After the show, Sting signed the guitar's body, and the bass was then offered as a prize in a listener's competition. The Precision came packed in its own stout flight case.

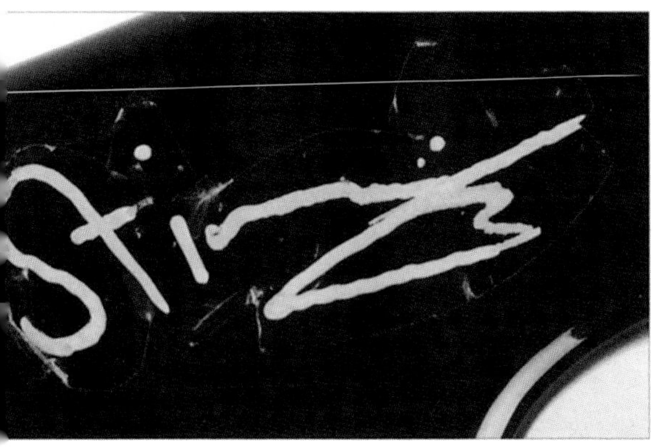

A florid Sting signature graces the upper bass bout of the Precision. The instrument was supplied in a flight case carrying a sticker which says "Play it? I can hardly carry it!"

Fender Custon Shop Jaguar Strat

This Fender Custom Shop Stratocaster dates from 1999, and is one of a limited edition of only 25 produced in partnership with Jaguar, Britain's world-famous sports car maker. The guitars are adorned with Jaguar logos, have a "British Racing Green" finish, and feature inlays and headstock facings crafted from walnut burl supplied by the automobile company's Coventry factory. Even their gig bags are made from the soft white leather used for Jaguar car seats.

The guitars have deluxe Fender features, including Lace Sensor pickups and gold hardware. The idea for the edition came from the late Ivor Arbiter, who headed Fender's UK distributor. This one was 24th in the series.

Fender Jag-Stang

Kurt Cobain of Nirvana was a devotee of both Fender Mustangs and Jaguars, and longed for a single guitar that would combine their best features. In 1993, he began to discuss what would become the Jag-Stang with Fender. Cobain cut up photographs of the two models, and stuck them together in the shape he wanted, with handwritten notes detailing neck dimension, pickup types, and finishes. Larry Brooks of Fender's Custom shop supervised the process of transforming these ideas into two finished instruments. Following the star's suicide in April 1994, it was decided to put the Jag-Stang into production, with the blessing of Kurt Cobain's family. It first appeared in 1991.

The Jag-Stang's neck (front) pickup is a Stratocaster-type unit; Kurt Cobain had originally asked for one from a Fender Mustang in this position. The guitar was designed to his specifications.

Fender Splatter Stratocaster

In summer 2003, Fender introduced a limited edition of Mexican-made Stratocasters with bizarre finishes. These were applied to the instruments' bodies and pickguards, prior to their necks and electronics being installed, by rotating them on turntables while spraying them with a combination of colored paints. The resultant swirls, blobs, and lines were sealed into the wood when its finish was applied.

The random nature of this operation meant that no two "paint jobs" were exactly the same. 3,000 "Splattercasters" were produced, selling for around $570. Under the finish, the Stratocasters were regular production instruments with alder bodies, maple necks and rosewood fingerboards.

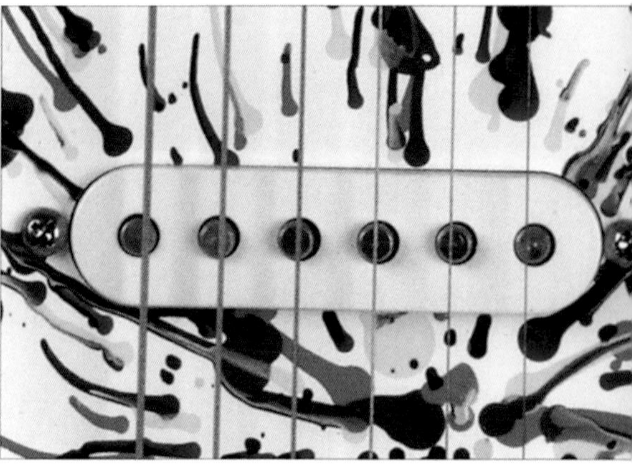

A close-up of the zany "splatter" finish created by rotating the bodies and pickguards on turntables prior to assembly.

Fret-King Country Squire

Trevor Wilkinson is one of the most respected figures in British and international guitar making circles, and his high quality vibratos, pickups and other hardware have been widely used in America and Europe for many years. Among Wilkinson's current projects is the Fret-King range of electrics: these began appearing in the late 1990s. The Country Squire shown here is Wilkinson's tribute to the Telecaster. It is produced in three versions. The one shown here is the "Classic," which has a solid two piece swamp ash body. It is in "Signal Red," and has Alnico V-type pickup units. The other Country Squires are the chambered "Semitone," and the Jeff Beck-inspired "Yardbird."

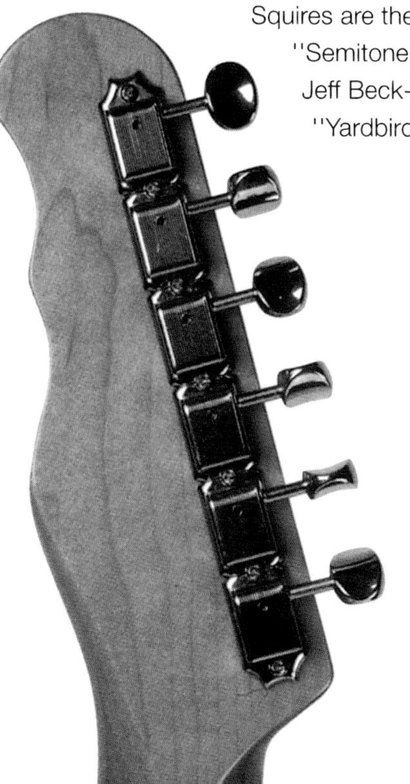

Fret-King Corona 60SP

The Fret-King Corona is described by its creator, Trevor Wilkinson, as a "homage to the classic double cutaway guitar of all time." This Fender Stratocaster-inspired design is available in three configurations, named 50, 60, and 70.

This example sports a "soapbar" pickup (with a look and sound reminiscent of Gibson's classic P-90 transducer) in its bridge position. 60s can also be supplied with humbuckers at their bridges, while the Corona 70 has them at both its neck and bridge. The 50 lacks these options, retaining a conventional Stratocaster-style pickup arrangement. All the Coronas have locking, height adjustable tuners, and Wilkinson/Gotoh VSV vibrato units.

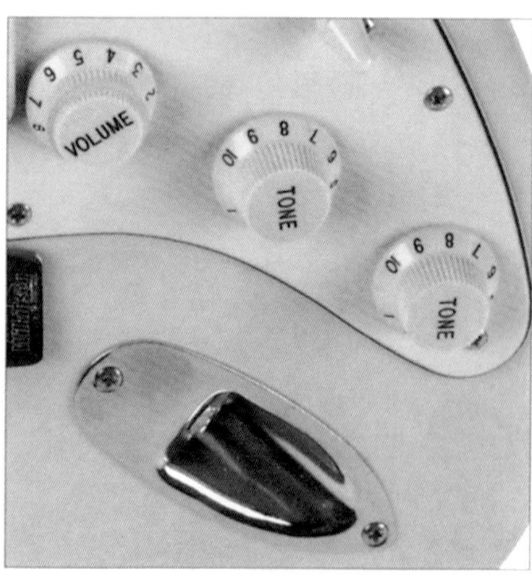

A detail of the contrasting cream pickguard with black beading, single volume control knob, tone knobs and recessed jack plug port.

Fury Bandit

The city of Saskatoon, in the Canadian province of Saskatchewan has been the home of Fury Guitars since 1962. The company was founded by instrument designer Glenn McDougall, and is still run by him and his wife, Janet. Glenn set up the company to start manufacturing the Fireball electric guitar he had been developing. He was unable to devote himself full time to lutherie until 1966.

The first decade of the new company's existence was "an uphill struggle," but many of the design features Glen developed during those early years are still found on today's Furys. Fury's current catalogue includes modernized versions of the Fireball and another 1960s model, the Fury Bandit.

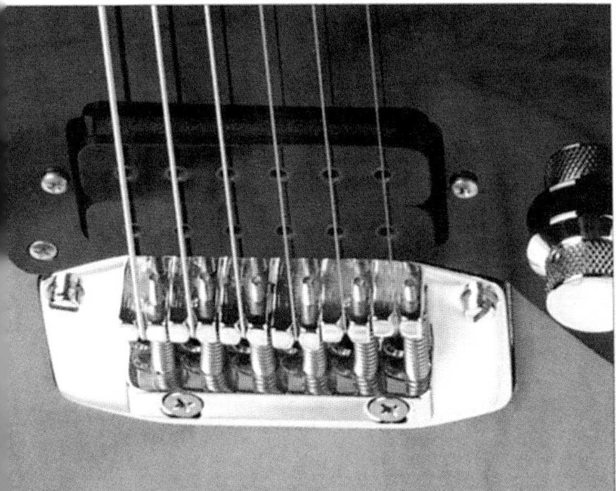

A detail of the Fury Bandit's tailpiece with the bottom humbucking pickup plus the chrome plated knurled volume knob that shows a fine attention to detail.

G & L F 100

G&L stands for "George & Leo." Leo Fender and his friend George Fullerton set up the company in 1980. They had recently left Music Man, and were seeking a new outlet for Leo's latest guitar innovations. G&L established itself in Fullerton, California, where the original Fender Electric Instrument Company had been based. The company's first product was the F-100 solid-body. This example dates from 1980. The instrument came in slightly different forms. This one is a Series 1 F-100E, which had a larger fingerboard radius (12 inch) than Series II models. The "E" suffix denotes active electronics, powered by an onboard battery. The series was produced until 1985.

The G&L logo as it appears on the headstock stands for George and Leo. Leo Fender went into business with his friend, George Fullerton, in 1980.

G & L ASAT Deluxe

Leo Fender worked at G&L for 11 years, until his death in 1991. Company ownership has now passed to BBE Sound. But, as one commentator put it, ''G&L has perpetuated the art of fine instrument making... in the distinguished tradition of its founder.'' Among the company most successful guitars are the ASATs, originally introduced in 1986, and still in production. Their curious name is said to refer to a chance remark from Leo Fender himself, that the instrument was conceived as ''a Strat and a Tele.''

Many top players, including Peter Frampton, INXS's Andrew, Tim Farriss, and the late Carl Perkins, have used them. This model is the Deluxe Semi-Hollow.

A detail of the fine figured maple finish and one of the instrument's two Seymour Duncan humbucking pickups which can be coil-tapped.

Gibson L-5 "Master Model"

Gibson was founded in Kalamazoo, Michigan in 1902, and was named for Orville Gibson (1856-1918), a master luthier with the company. His innovative mandolin and steel-strung guitar designs dominated Gibson's early catalogs. Gibson left in 1911, due to ill health. In 1919, Gibson recruited Lloyd Allayre Loar (1886-1943).

His designs, including the 1922 F-5 archtop mandolin (with f-holes), and the 1922 L-5 "Master Model" guitar were extremely important to both Gibson and guitar design itself. The latter is recognized as the basis for almost all subsequent archtop acoustic designs. It had f-holes, a carved top and back, and a handsomely finished 16-inch wide body.

The L-5s black pickguard is finely bound in contrasting white edging and supported by an adjustable strut.

Gibson Super 400

Although Lloyd Loar resigned from Gibson in 1924, the company continued its pioneering design work. 1934 saw the appearance of an impressive new model, the Super 400. This instrument had several striking features: its $400 price tag, its glamorous appearance, and its great, 18-inch width. This was intended to give the guitar extra volume. The Super 400 was adopted by several high-profile players, but remained beyond the reach of most musicians in the Depression. Relatively few were made, and it has become one of the most iconic Gibsons of the 1930s. Epiphone and Stromberg of Boston, Massachusetts subsequently constructed even wider guitars.

The Super 400's pickguard is available in a faux marble finish with a white bound edging and has an adjustable strut for support.

Gibson L-5 Cutaway

Gibson launched another important model in 1934, a new version of its L-5 archtop. It now had a 17-inch body. As rivalry been archtop manufacturers grew more intense, the hunt was on for additional features that could increase market share.

One such innovation was the cutaway body, invented by Gibson, and introduced as an option of the L-5 and Super 400 models in 1939. As a contemporary ad explained, this "Gibson First" provided scope for "more notes, more chords, [and] faster, smoother runs." The concept proved extremely successful, and cutaway models were soon outselling conventional archtops. Other companies were soon offering cutaway models of their own.

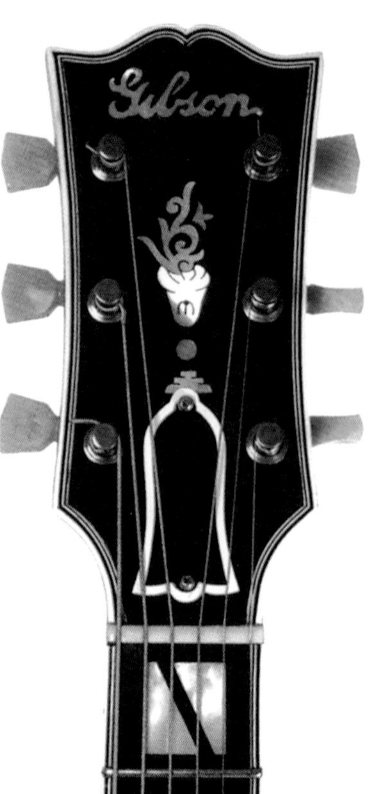

Gibson ES-150

Early electric guitars were ''Hawaiian'' models, designed to be laid horizontally on the player's lap. Gibson introduced its first ''Electric Spanish''-style 6-string standard guitar. The ES-150 was a 161⁄4-inch wide model with a solid spruce arched top, maple back and sides, and a single ''bar-type'' pickup. Its entry in the company's catalog contained some words of advice for would-be purchasers unfamiliar with electric instruments.

They were told to ''strike the strings lightly and you [will] have a tone that can be amplified to any volume you desire.'' Electric guitars swiftly caught on among performers. ES-150 user Charlie Christian joined the Benny Goodman Orchestra in 1939.

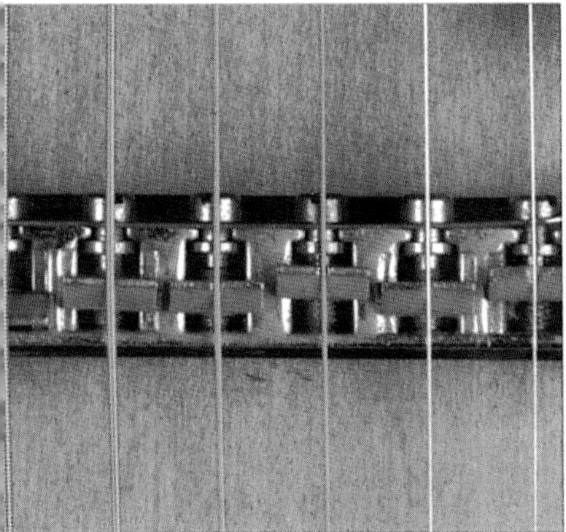

This adjustable bridge on this 1950s model is considerably more elaborate than the basic wooden unit fitted to the ES-150s that were produced by Gibson between 1936 and 1942.

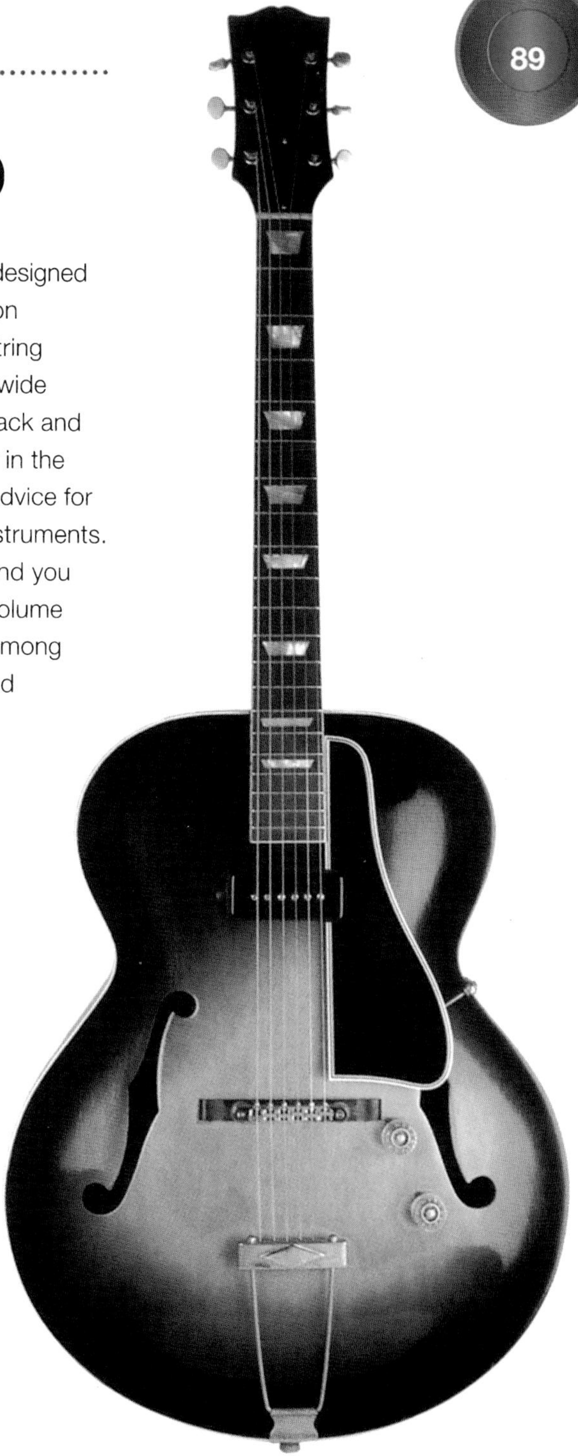

Gibson ES-175D

Whereas the ES-150 was launched as a solid-timbered archtop in the 1930s, and "reborn" in a laminated version after World War II, the (1949) ES-175 had a plywood body from the start. This was in line with most of Gibson's electric hollow-bodies. It also had a cutaway, a feature not found on the pre-war Gibsons. "175" reflected the model's original price of $175. The first 175s were fitted with a single P-90 pickup, and a relatively plain, trapeze-type tailpiece. 1953 saw a two-pickup model, the ES-175D.

Humbuckers appeared in 1957. The 175 has been described as "one of Gibson's ultimate bread-and-butter instruments," in continuous production since 1949.

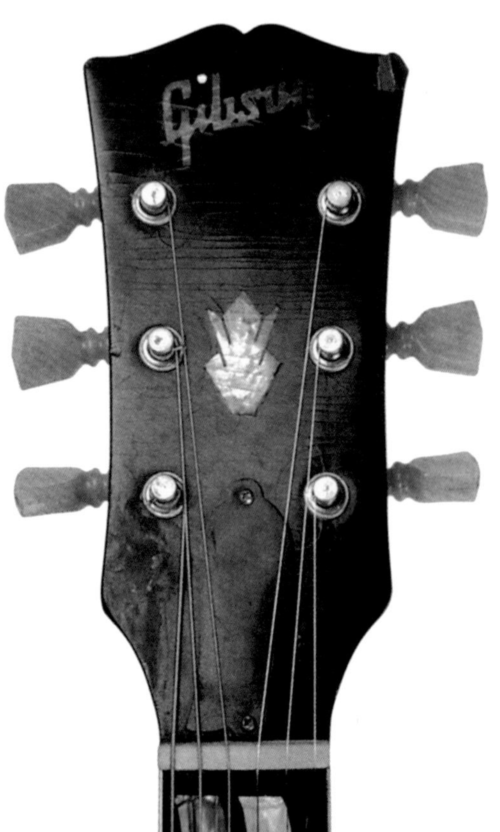

Gibson ES-140

Though a thriving market existed for reduced-size acoustic guitars suitable for children and small-handed musicians, no scaled-down electrics were available until the Gibson ES-140 debuted in 1950. The 140 was a three-quarter size version of the ES-175, and had similar equipment.

It went on to sell very well, and was endorsed by the likes of 1950s child star Larry Collins, half of the Oklahoma-based Collins Kids rockabilly duo. Earlier ES-140s, such as this one (which dates from 1955), had a 33⁄8 inch body depth (as did the original ES-175), but this was slimmed down to 13⁄4 inches in 1956. The guitar was the renamed the ES-140T, and produced in this form until 1968.

The Gibson ES-140 has a maple body, with a rosewood bridge and a trapeze tailpiece. Its neck is made from mahogany.

Gibson ES-295

The Gibson ES-295 debuted in 1952. Gibson called it a "golden beauty," a "royal instrument," and asserted that "tone and action wise the ES-295 measures up to its outstanding appearance." Visually, the elegant new archtop matched Gibson's Les Paul solid-body. But it bore a close resemblance to the ES-175, with the same overall dimensions, "Florentine" cutaways, and "parallelogram" fret markers.

All three models featured P-90 single-coil pickups. The ES-295 never became a bestseller, and was dropped in 1958. But it has an enduring place in musical history, as the guitar used by Elvis Presley sideman Scotty Moore on "That's All Right" and "Blue Moon of Kentucky."

The "flower" decoration on the ES-295's pickguard had been seen before on a Gibson lap steel.

Gibson L-5 CES

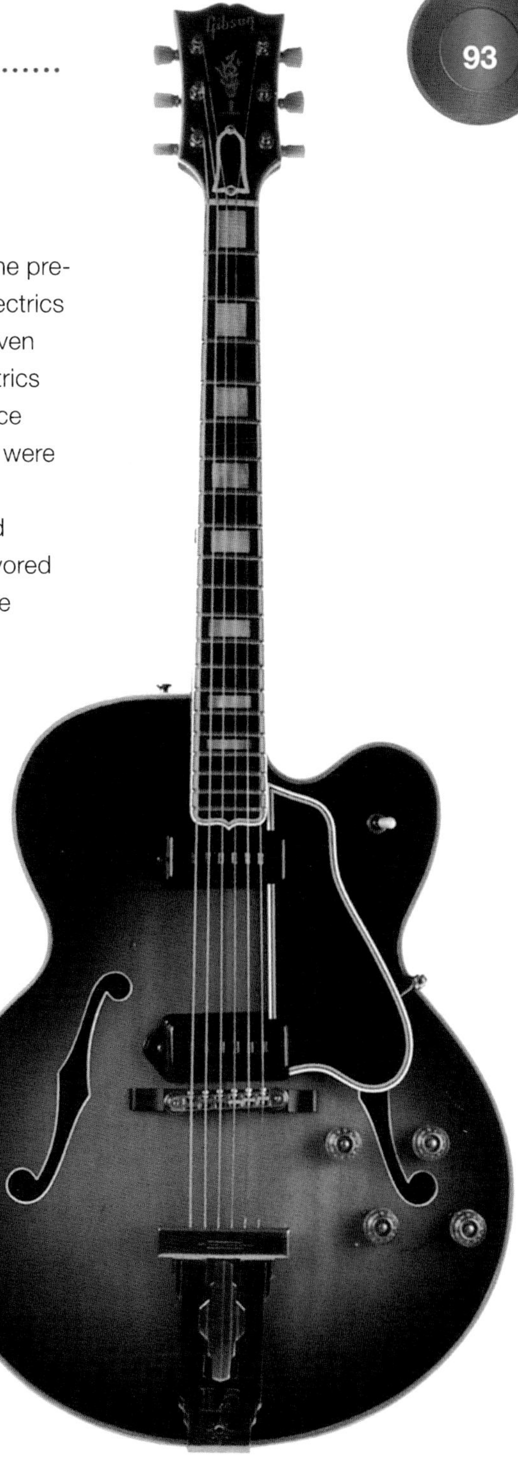

Gibson's two flagship archtop acoustic models of the pre-war period, the L-5 and Super 400, appeared as electrics in 1951. They kept their original names, but were given the suffix CES (Cutaway Electric Spanish). The electrics retained their all-solid wood construction, with spruce tops, and solid maple back and sides. But the tops were built slightly thicker, and were more heavily braced. This was to give the instruments greater rigidity, and avoid any unwanted vibration. Both guitars were favored by leading jazzmen, including Wes Montgomery. The original P-90 pickups were swapped for Alnico V transducers in 1954 (as seen on this model), and, later, by humbuckers.

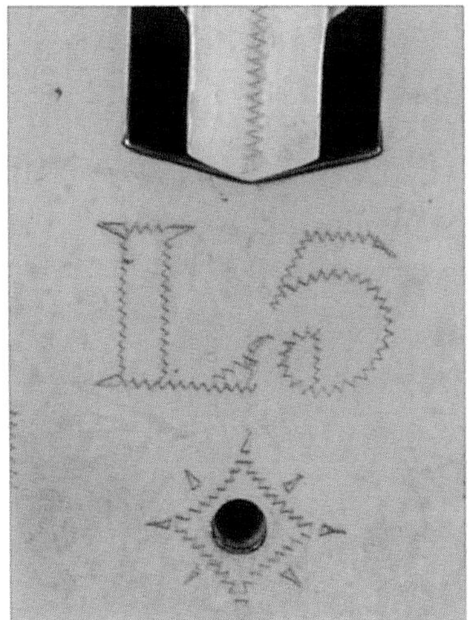

This ornate plated metal trapeze tailpiece with L5 embossed on it closely resembles one fitted to the pre-war models.

Gibson Byrdland

When two leading Nashville-based players, Billy Byrd (1920-2001) and Hank Garland (1930-2004), were invited to discuss guitar design with a Gibson representation in early 1955, they suggested that the company should come up with what Garland later described as "an instrument like the L-5, but with a thin body and a bunch of other stuff."

The Gibson Byrdland was launched later that same year. Although the guitar was based on the L-5 CES, it was just 2¼ inches deep. It also had a slightly shorter scale length and a narrower neck. It was described as "streamlined," and successfully combined the best characteristics of solid body and conventional designs.

This example of the Byrdland has had its original tailpiece (which carried the model's name) replaced with a Bigsby vibrato unit.

Gibson ES-335

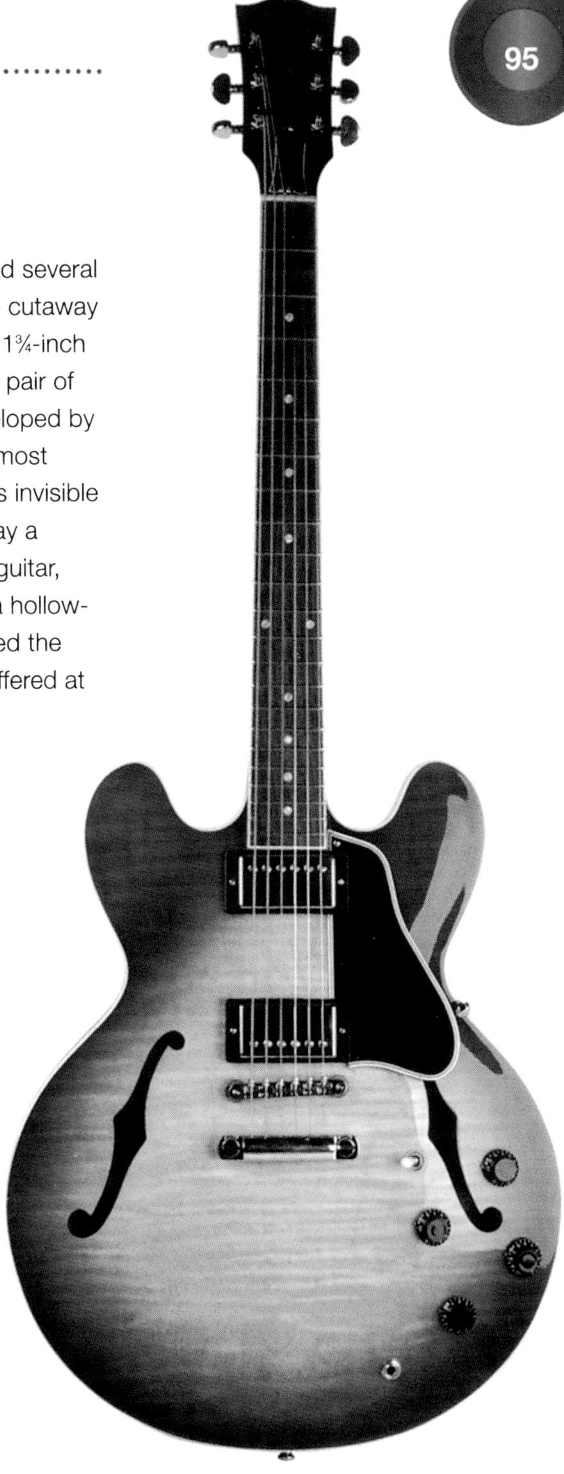

Gibson's ES-335, introduced in spring 1958, had several immediately striking features, including a double cutaway (a first for the company), a thinline body (whose 1¾-inch depth matched that of the 1955 ES-225), and a pair of "patent applied for" humbucking pickups, developed by staff engineer Seth Lover (1910-1997). But the most revolutionary aspect of the ES-335's design was invisible from outside: beneath its laminated maple top lay a wooden block that ran lengthways through the guitar, transforming what would otherwise have been a hollow-body into a "semi-solid." This drastically reduced the feedback from which many electric archtops suffered at

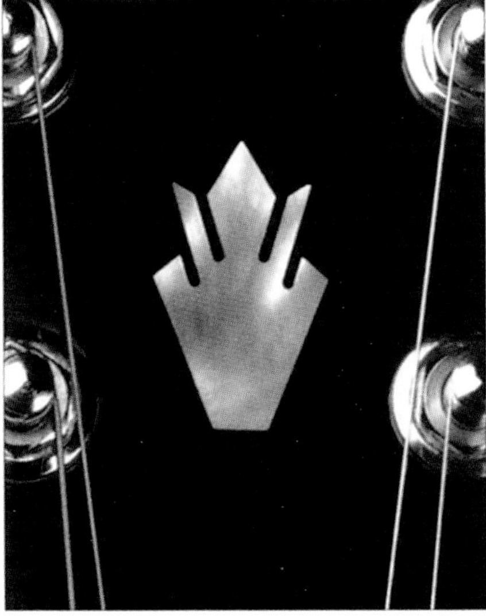

The inset mother-of-pearl crown on the headstock; this is mounted at a 17-degree angle to optimize the instrument's tone quality.

Gibson ES-335 (2)

In 1962, Gibson made a purely cosmetic change to the ES-335, substituting block inlays for its "dot" fingerboard markers. A rather more significant alternation occurred some two years later, with the replacement of the model's "stop" or "stud" tailpiece with a trapeze-type unit. This 335 dates from 1968, and has been owned by British jazz guitarist Charles Alexander since the late 1970s. His previous Gibson, a stereo-equipped ES-345 was stolen.

The solid center block gives the instrument a contemporary sustain than the more "retro" timbre obtained from a hollow-body electric. The guitar is also equipped with a bridge pickup, but Alexander prefers to use the neck transducer.

A detail of this model's "trapeze" tailpiece, which is an alternative to the "stop" or "stud" tailpiece shown on the ES-335 on the previous page.

Gibson EB-2 Bass

The Gibson EB-2 first appeared in 1958; like the visually similar ES-335 guitar launched the same year, it contained an internal center block to improve sustain and reduce feedback. Initially fitted with a single-coil pickup, it had acquired a humbucker by 1959.

It was also equipped with the ''sensational Gibson Bass-Baritone switch,'' a tone circuit giving an additional ''edge'' to the instrument's sound. The same feature was included on the Epiphone Rivoli, an EB-2 lookalike that also debuted in 1959. The EB-2 itself was dropped in 1961, but returned three years later, and 1966 saw the appearance of the 2-pickup version seen here. Both basses remained available until the early 1970s.

The Gibson logo on the pickguard has worn away with forty years of hard rocking.

Gibson ES-345TD

The Gibson ES-345TD was introduced in 1959. While similar in construction and appearance to the ES-335, it had two novel features: stereo wiring, and ''Vari-tone'' circuitry. According to the company's publicity, Vari-tone ''could produce any sound you've ever heard from any guitar.'' Vari-tone settings are adjusted via a rotary knob mounted to the left of the instrument's volume and tone controls. This has six positions. Many players find it useful, and consider that positions 3 and 4 can make the ES-345's humbucking pickups sound a little like single-coil models. The guitar also had stereo capabilities that meant it could use Gibson's own GA-885 stereo guitar amp.

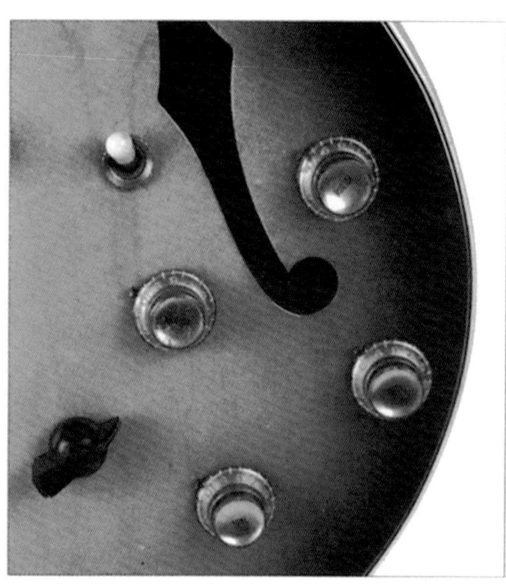

The 345's black Bakelite Vari-tone switch normally has a circular surround but it appears to be missing from this example.

Gibson ES-355TD-SV

The ES-355TD-SV ("Thinline Double-cutaway Stereo Vari-tone") was launched in 1959. It was a luxury reworking of the ES-335 that also featured the stereo wiring and Vari-tone circuitry found on the ES-345. It inspired extreme adulation, being described as a "magnificent jazz guitar reflect[ing] all the beauty and skill of the guitar maker's art." It is indeed a handsome instrument that inspired many devoted followers. Among its famous players were top Nashville session player Grady Martin, jazzman Tony Mottola, and blues star B. B. King. Like all his instruments, King named his ES-355 Lucille. He later switched to a version with a sealed top to prevent feedback.

Gibson ES-5 Switchmaster, 1959

The major selling point for the original Gibson ES-5, which debuted in 1949, was its unusual pickup configuration. Named "the instrument of a thousand voices," it boasted three P-90s, each with its own volume knob. However, there was no selector switch for the transducers, and only a single, overall tone control. Opinion was divided over the efficacy of this arrangement, and Gibson altered the circuitry in 1955. The new model, the Switchmaster, was also provided with a selector, providing individual tone controls for the pickups. In 1957, humbucking pickups replaced the P-90s. This is an example of the revamped version of the Switchmaster from 1959.

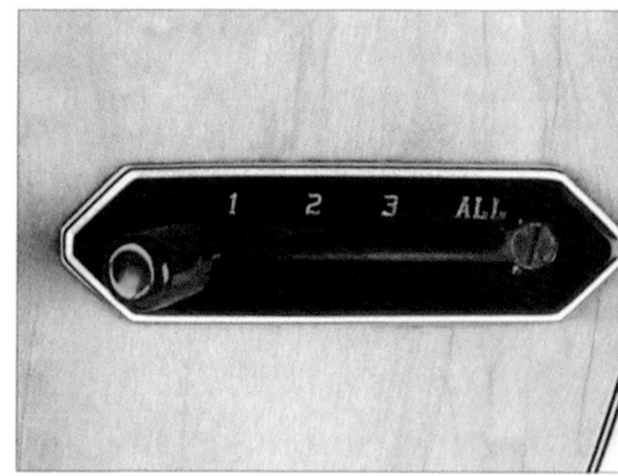

The provision of a pickup selector on the ES-5 was widely welcomed giving its name the "Switchmaster." The slider switch positioned on the lower bout allows selection of pickups 1,2,3 or all of them!

Gibson ES-5 Switchmaster, 1961

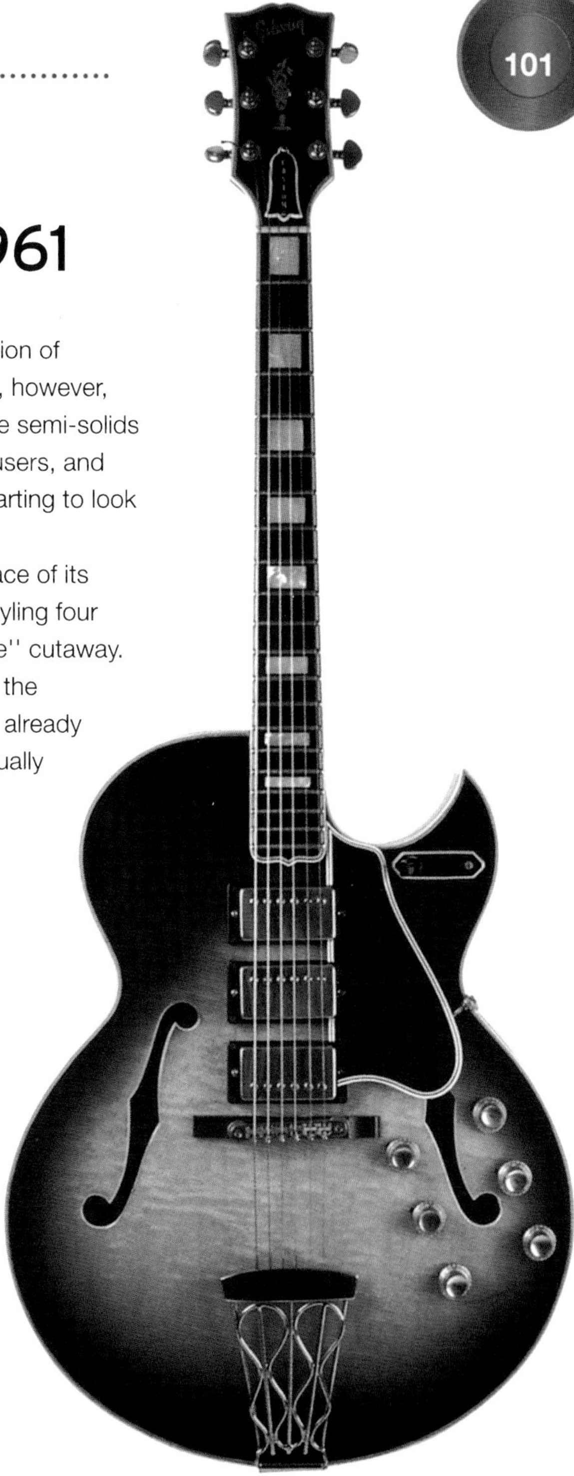

The ES-5 heralded the start of the new generation of Gibson instruments. By the end of that decade, however, the instrument's future was less certain. Thinline semi-solids were now the choice of many Gibson archtop users, and the bulky, though elegant Switchmaster was starting to look and sound dated.

It had been given humbucking pickups in place of its P-90s in 1957, and it underwent a change in styling four years later, when it acquired a sharp "Florentine" cutaway. However, by the time this alteration was made, the number of Switchmasters being produced was already beginning to dwindle, and the guitar was eventually discontinued in 1962. This is a 1961 model.

Gibson ES-120T

Demand for the "thinline" electric archtops introduced by Gibson in 1955 grew steadily over the following years, and in 1962, the company added a budget-price model to the series, the ES-120T, which sold at just under $150.

It shared its body dimensions and some aspects of its styling with the ES-125T, the former "bottom-of-the-range" thinline (introduced in 1956). But the new guitar had one significant difference. On the 120T, the 125's P-90 transducer was replaced with a combined pickguard-and-pickup similar to the one found on the Melody Maker. Because all the wiring and controls were mounted on a plastic plate, there were no electronics within the guitar's body.

The thinline hollowbody ES-120T has only a single unbound f-hole in its maple laminate top.

Gibson L-5 CES, 1963

Some guitars enjoy only a brief period in the limelight, but the Gibson L-5, whose original acoustic version dates back to 1922, is a hardy perennial. Unlike other classic archtops, its status and sales were largely untouched by the changes in taste that affected almost everything in the 1960s.

It retained a place in the Gibson catalog throughout that decade, and beyond. Technically, however, changes were made to the instrument. By the later 1950s, its single-coil Alnico V pickups had given way to the Seth Lover designed humbuckers. Another new feature, the sharper Florentine cutaway, that replaced the softer Venetian one in around 1960, led to the shortening of the L-5's pickguard.

Every care went into the L-5's headstock, which has intricate decorative inlays and gold-plated tuners and nuts.

Gibson L-5, Custom Order 1964

The concept of a ''custom shop'' was still unknown to guitar makers and buyers in the early 1960s, largely because manufacturers (even major ones such as Gibson) were still able to accommodate special orders and modifications as part of their production process. An unknown musician commissioned this unusual L-5 1964. His requirements were relatively simple. He preferred a Venetian cutaway to the usual Florentine type, and asked for a bar-style single-coil pickup to be fitted instead of the usual humbucker.

This preference suggests that he might have been a devotee of Charlie Christian, the 150's most famous user. All the pre-war ES-150s were so equipped.

The L-5 Custom Order's gold-plated bridge permits precise adjustments to be made for individual strings.

Gibson Howard Roberts Fusion

Following the reintroduction of the Howard Roberts Custom, Gibson continued to collaborate with the distinguished jazzman (who was known as an enthusiastic modifier of his own instruments). 1979 saw the launch of a new Roberts model, the Fusion. Its single-cutaway outline is reminiscent of the ES-175, one of the guitars Roberts used regularly before acquiring his "signature" Epiphone.

However, the Fusion is both narrower and shallower than the 175, and lacks its hollow body, featuring an ES-335-like solid center section instead. This example is an early Fusion, without some of the refinements that Gibson and Roberts were to add later. Howard died of cancer in 1992.

The TP-6 bridge/tailpiece allows tuning adjustment on this 1980 model, but it was replaced on later Fusions.

Gibson Howard Roberts Custom

Howard Roberts (1929-1992) was a famous session guitarist of the 1950s and 60s, based in Los Angeles. He was especially in demand for movie and TV soundtracks, but his first love was always jazz. Roberts was also an innovative teacher, and co-founded the prestigious Guitar Institute of Technology. In 1961, Chicago Musical Instruments (who owned both Gibson and Epiphone), invited Roberts to develop a new semi-acoustic that would bear his name.

The resultant instrument debuted as an Epiphone in 1964. It was discontinued in 1970, but reappeared as a Gibson in 1974. This guitar dates from this time. It is essentially similar to the Epiphone version of the instrument.

The unusually shaped fingerboard inlays on this 1970s model also appeared on the original Epiphone Howard Roberts Custom.

Gibson ES-135

In its original incarnation, the Gibson ES-135 was a non-cutaway archtop with a single pickup: it debuted in 1954, but spent only four years in the catalog. The 135 seen here, first introduced in 1991, is an entirely different instrument with combines the outline of an ES-175 (with its distinctive Florentine cutaway), and the shallow body and internal center block of an ES-335. Its two pickups are Gibson P-100s, ''stacked humbuckers'' based on the classic P-90 design, but with an additional, noise-eliminating coil.

The new guitar was immediately successful, and, in 200, was honoured with an ''Editors' Pick'' award from the influential magazine Guitar Player.

A detail shows the black hardware that contrasts well with the ''Cherry'' paintjob, and shows the P-100 humbucking pickups that are noted for their throaty power and sustain.

Gibson Les Paul 1956 Replica

Les Paul (born Lester William Polfus, 1915) has a special place in the history of the electric guitar. A brilliant player, he also took an active interest in guitar design. After a series of abortive discussions with commercial guitar makers, including Leo Fender, Les agreed to collaborate with Gibson on a mass-production solid-body electric that would bear his name.

The elegantly shaped, gold-topped Gibson Les Paul appeared in 1952. It was described as "the instrument everyone has been waiting for." Gibson president Ted McCarty and his team of designers and craftsmen were heavily involved in the design of the new guitar. This is a Gibson Custom Shop replica of the 1956 version.

This 1956 replica is fitted with Gibson P-90 single-coil pickups. Below the P-90 are the adjustable bridge and "stud" or "stop" tailpiece.

Gibson Les Paul Custom

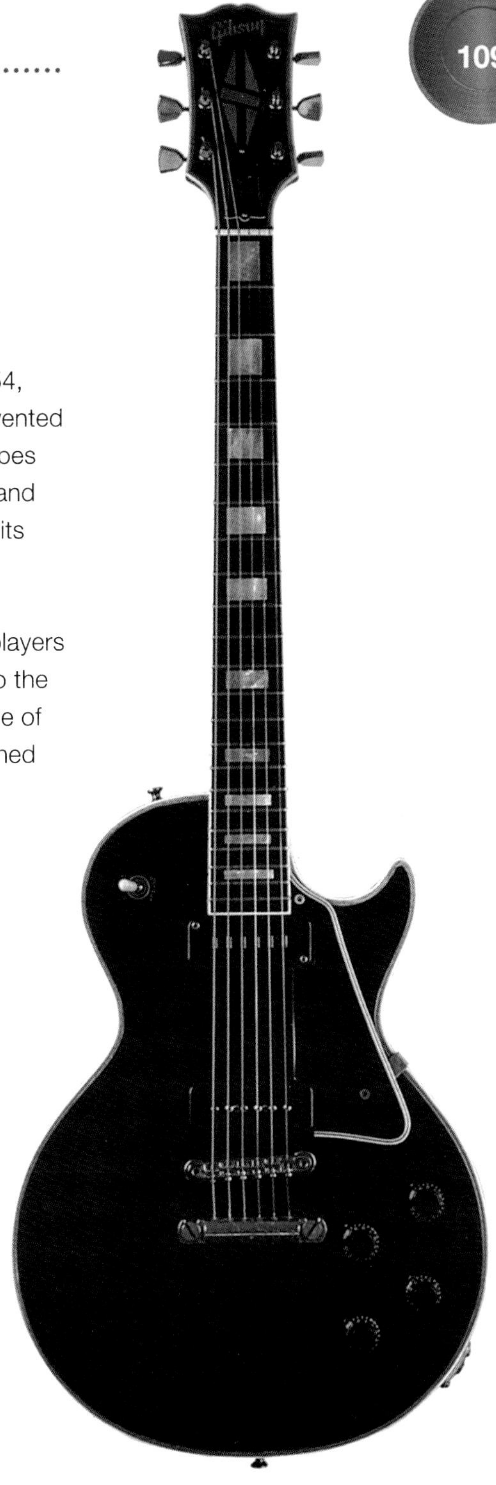

The Les Paul Custom started out as an upgrade to Gibson's original Les Paul model. Introduced in 1954, it featured the adjustable "Tune-o-Matic" bridge invented by Ted McCarty, and was fitted with two different types of single-coil pickup: a P-90 in the bridge position, and an Alnico V, named for the type of magnet used for its pole-pieces, near its neck.

Gibson engineer Seth Lover's Alnico transducer offered high output, but performed less well when players raised its height excessively. Its all-black finish led to the nickname "Black Beauty," while the low, wide profile of its frets, which made fast left-hand work easier, earned it the soubriquet "Fretless Wonder."

The Custom's neck with its sleek ebony fingerboard is elegant as well as fast-playing.

Gibson Les Paul Standard

In 1957, both the gold-top and Custom Gibson Les Pauls acquired new pickups, the twin-coil, "humbucking" transducers developed a few years earlier by staffer Seth Lover. The rich timbre provided by these units has come to be widely regarded as the "classic Les Paul sound," although some players retain a preference for the P-90s and Alnicos fitted to earlier models.

In 1958, the instrument's gold finish was replaced with a sunburst look, and it was renamed the Les Paul Standard. In the initial production years of 1958-60, only 1,700 Standards were made, and became almost mythical. They were discontinued to make way for Gibson's new SG-shaped solid-bodies.

A close-up of one of the large twin-coil humbucking pickups, showing the distinctive pinkish cream-colored surrounds that characterize the Standard.

Gibson Melody Maker

Eager to capture a share of the market for less expensive electric guitars as well as premium models, Gibson launched a budget-priced Les Paul in 1954. Named the Junior, it sold for just $99.50, and was fitted with a single P-90 pickup; a 3⁄4-size version appeared two years later. 1959 saw the introduction of a new Gibson solid-body, also priced at $99.50.

Christened the Melody Maker, it bore a strong resemblance to the single-cutaway Junior, although its body was slightly thinner than its predecessor's, while its headstock was narrower, and its pickup assemble was an all-in-one unit built into it pickguard. The Les Pauls were now moving towards becoming SGs.

This narrow headstock, just 2¼ inches wide, is a distinctive feature of the Gibson Melody Maker.

Gibson Flying V

By the mid-1950s, the success of the Fender Telecaster and Stratocaster was making Gibson look like "a fuddy duddy old company without a new idea in years." To silence such comments, McCarty urgently needed to come up with some fresh, bold designs.

By 1957, he had devised modernistic body shapes for three radical-looking solid electrics, the Moderne, the Futura (soon to be renamed the Explorer), and the Flying V. The Flying V and Explorer were unveiled to industry insiders at trade fairs in 1957, and went into production in 1958. Initial sales were disappointing, and the Flying V was temporarily dropped from the Gibson catalog only a year later. This example is from 2002.

On earlier Flying Vs, the "Gibson" logo was placed on the headstock; here, it has migrated to the truss rod cover.

Gibson SG Custom

Since its first appearance in 1952, the single-cutaway Gibson Les Paul has been highly successful. By the early 1960s, however, sales were declining, as demand grew for lighter-bodied, more streamlined types of electric such as the Fender Stratocaster. The bosses at Kalamazoo responded by giving their Les Pauls a makeover. A 3-pickup Les Paul Custom was introduced in 1961, with a narrower, contoured body with two sharp-horned cutaways.

The model's new features included a vibrato and a choice of finishes. The ''fretless wonder'' neck was retained. By 1963, the Les Paul name had vanished from the company's guitars, as ''Les Pauls'' were renamed ''Solid Guitars'' (''SGs'').

This ornately engraved solid tailpiece seems a little out of place on the face-lifted contoured solid body which the Kalamazoo company hoped would help them to compete with the likes of Fender.

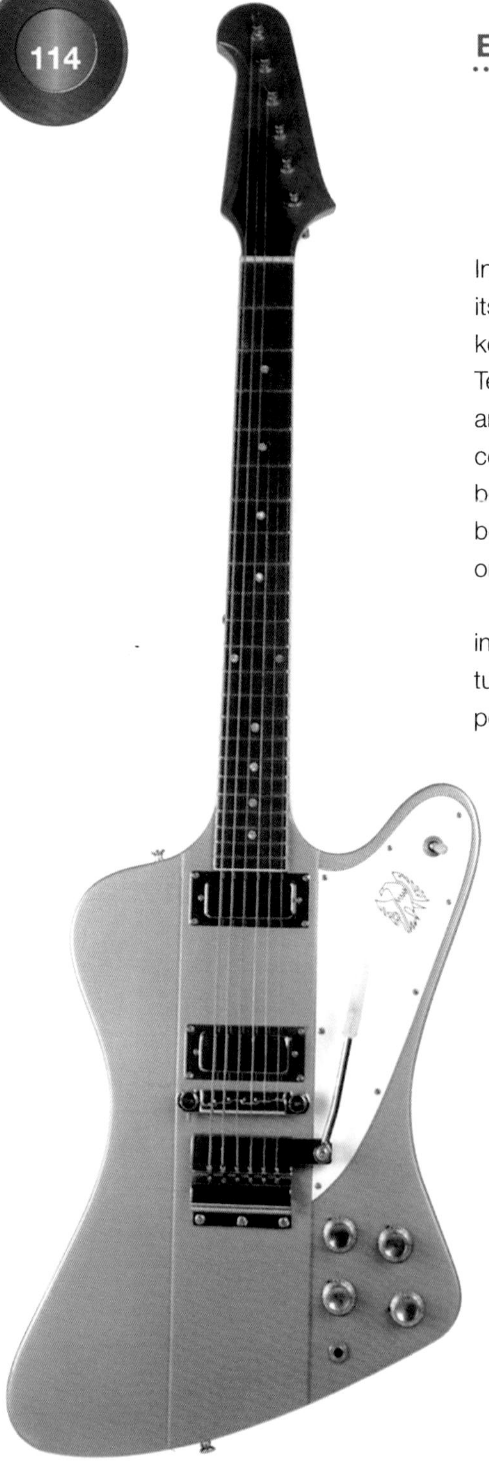

Gibson Firebird III

In the early 1960s, Gibson turned to a surprising source in its search for bold, "cutting-edge" solid-body designs to keep up the pressure on its rivals. The company's boss, Ted McCarty, admired the work of automotive engineer and stylist Ray Dietrich (1894-1980), and invited him to contribute to the development of a radical new guitar, to be named the Firebird. Dietrich's Firebirds were "reverse bodied" (with their treble horns longer than their bass ones).

He also gave them a "neck-through-body" construction instead of a conventional glued-in or bolted-on neck. He turned their headstocks around, and fitted mirror-image pegheads. The Firebirds were launched in 1963.

Automobile engineer and stylist, Ray Dietrich, designed the famous Firebird logo that is positioned on the guitar's pickguard.

Gibson Firebird V

The Gibson Firebirds were not especially well received by dealers or customers, and Fender asserted that the shape infringed its copyright of the Jazzmaster and Jaguar designs. Gibson made some major changes to the range in 1965. The guitars' reverse bodies and headstocks were abandoned, sideways-mounted tuners were fitted, and the "neck-through-body" construction was replaced with a standard neck joint.

There were also some hardware changes: the P-90 pickups were substituted for humbuckers on the Firebird I and III. By 1969, the vamped models were dropped. But affection for the original Firebirds led to several revivals and reissues. This recently made Firebird V has the original "reverse" features.

Gibson EB-0 Bass, 1959

The mahogany-bodied, short-scale Gibson EB-0 bass was introduced in 1959 at a retail price of $195, and early examples (like this one) share the body outline of the Les Paul Junior 6-string guitar. The late 50s and early 60s saw frequent changes in the Gibson's specifications, and the guitar survived for only two years in its original form. It was re-styled in 1961 (to match the SG guitar), and a companion model, the EB-3 was launched. This had two pickups. A string mute was added to the EB-0, and a long-scale (301/2-inch) version debuted in 1969. The EB-0 remained in production until 1979. This instrument formerly belonged to Jim Kale of the Canadian band Guess Who, who charted with "American Woman."

The EB-Os headstock is decorated with the Gibson logo and a crown. Both are inlayed.

Gibson Pete Townshend SG

Peter Townshend of the Who has used (and abused!) many different guitars during his long career, but is most closely associated with the Gibson SG Special. The SG range went through numerous changes followed its introduction in 1961, but Townshend's principle onstage "axes" throughout the late 60s and early 70s were post-1966 Specials. Produced in "Cherry Red" and "Polaris White" they had pickguards that completely surrounded their twin P-90 single coil pickups.

The factory-fitted vibrato units proved too fragile to withstand his heavy right-hand "power chording," and he invariably removed them. The original SG Specials were discontinued in 1971, but a limited edition was produced in 2000.

The chrome tuner buttons have been deliberately tarnished to make the guitar look like a 1970s relic.

Gibson Les Paul Custom, 1978

The old-style, single-cutaway Gibson Les Paul Custom had retained a firm following among many musicians. By the mid-1960s, second-hand examples, such as the one purchased by Eric Clapton in New York in 1967, were fetching high prices. The company responded by re-introducing the pre-SG "Black Beauty" and the Les Paul Standard in 1968.

Keen to capitalize on the instrument's enduring popularity, Gibson subsequently produced it in a range of different colors, and has gone on to mark the milestones in its long life with various "Special" models. This "Natural" two-pickup Custom dates from 1978.

Neck (front) and bridge (back) pickups are termed (respectively) "rhythm" and "treble," as shown on the Les Paul selector switch.

Gibson EDS-1275

The Gibson EDS-1275 6- and 12-string doubleneck electrics debut in 1958. Originally a hollow-body instrument, it was restyled as an SG-type solid by 1962. Gibson described the Double 12 as a "completely new and exciting instrument," and adventurous guitarists relished the opportunity to switch, effortlessly, between its necks, or use them simultaneously.

These included UK "prog-rocker" Steve Howe of Yes and Charlie Whitney of Family, while the 1275's best-known exponent was Jimmy Page of Led Zeppelin. The EDS-1275's size and weight may limit its appeal, but it remains the world's only instantly recognizable doubleneck, and has a special place in the history of rock.

To avoid a confusing proliferation of knobs, the 1275 has only overall volume and tone controls for the pickups on each of its necks.

Gibson L-5S

Gibson's famous L-5 model had already been produced as an acoustic and electric archtop, but in 1972 it appeared as a solid. The L-5S, as it was termed, boasted an elegant maple body, a "Cherry Sunburst" finish (other color options were added later), and two low impedance pickups similar to the type previously used on certain late 1960s and early 1970s Les Pauls.

Despite the "Custom" legend on its truss-rod cover, the L-5S was actually a regular, production model. It was also one of the comparatively few models still being built at Gibson's original factory in Kalamazoo, Michigan. This L-5S was made in 1978, and was previously the property of Queen vocalist Paul Rodgers.

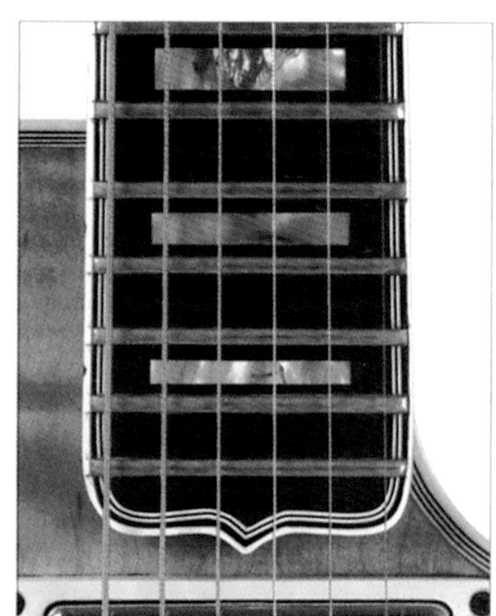

This close-up reveals the fancy binding around the L-5S's ebony fingerboard, whose pointed end has been a feature of L-5 design since the 1920s.

Gibson Les Paul Bass

The first Gibson Les Paul bass appeared in 1970. Like the Les Paul "Personal" 6-string guitar that debuted the previous year, it utilized low impedance circuitry, which offered greatly reduced background noise and an extended frequency response. Gibson's LP bass had "crisp, clear tones [that would] exceed [those] of any electric bass on the market to date." These models enjoyed only limited success although both remained in the catalog until 1979.

There were no more Les Paul basses until the 1990s. This Les Paul Bass was described as combining "a classic look and solid performance with basic functionality." This finish is "Ebony," but it is also available in "Classic White."

The adjustable tail end of a bass with a 34-inch scale, an ebony fingerboard, and a nut width of 1 1/16 inches.

Gibson Grabber Bass

In 1973, Gibson's L9-S bass appeared, but within a year, had been given a more memorable, not to say aggressive new name, the Ripper. This was the start of a trend for Gibsons with a gutsy image. The next bass to come out of Kalamazoo was the Grabber, launched in 1974. Unlike the previous basses, the Grabber had a bolt-on neck. It had an alder body and a maple neck and fingerboard.

Its other striking features included a pickup that players could slide up or down to alter the tone it produced, and a very distinctively pointed headstock. This was replicated on the Maurader 6-string electric, which appeared the following year in 1975. The Grabber remained in Gibson's catalog until 1982.

Gibson 'The Paul'

In the late 1970s, Gibson unveiled its ''Firebrand'' series of electric guitars. This consisted of lower-cost, stripped-down versions of some of the company's most famous designs. The standard ''Paul'' shown here dates from 1979. Its body is cut from a piece of mahogany, without the maple ''crown'' found on instruments such as the Les Paul Standard or Custom, and it has little in the way of visual refinement; even the ''Gibson'' logo is ''burned'' into the wood of its headstock instead of being inlaid. The neck was walnut, the fingerboard ebony.

The regular ''Paul'' was available from 1978 until 1982; its deluxe cousin appeared in 1980, and survived until 1986. Neither has been revived.

The rear side of the headstock reveals Grover machine head tuners and serial number stamped direct into the walnut.

Gibson Les Paul, 2002

The proliferation of Les Pauls in the current Gibson catalog provides a vast range of choices for players, whether their preference is for vintage-style models, or for striking new versions of the classic solid-body. The instrument shown here falls into the latter category. A Les Paul Standard Mahogany, dating for 2002, it lacks the maple top found on earlier Standards, and also departs from tradition by having three pickups instead of two.

Standard Mahogany guitars of this type are no longer produced by Gibson, and are something of a rarity. This model has a "Heritage Cherry" finish is used for the Heritage Special's carved top and body. The neck is also mahogany.

A detail of one of the three Distortion Humbuckers supplied by Seymour Duncan of Santa Barbara, California.

Gibson BluesHawk

Gibson's "Hawk" series of electric guitars was born in 1993, when the solid-body, single cutaway NightHawk made its debut. It attracted a considerable following (high-profile users included Joe Walsh of The Eagles), and three years later, the BluesHawk augmented the range. This was thinline, hollow-body design fitted with two Gibson "Blues 90" pickups.

These incorporated a dummy coil to reduce noise and interference, and produced an impressive range of sounds, especially when used in conjunction with the NightHawk's Varitone tone selector. After being switched into circuit by pulling up the tone control, this could then be adjusted, via a rotary knob below the pickup selector.

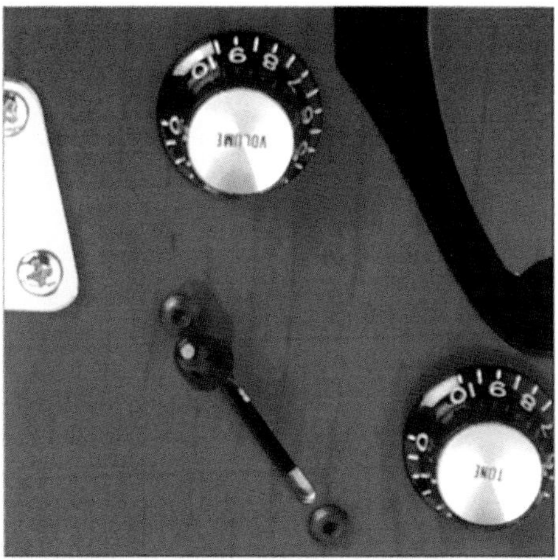

The Gibson's thinline, hollow-body design is constructed in poplar for the back and sides and maple (seen here) for the top. The colored varnish lets the grain show through.

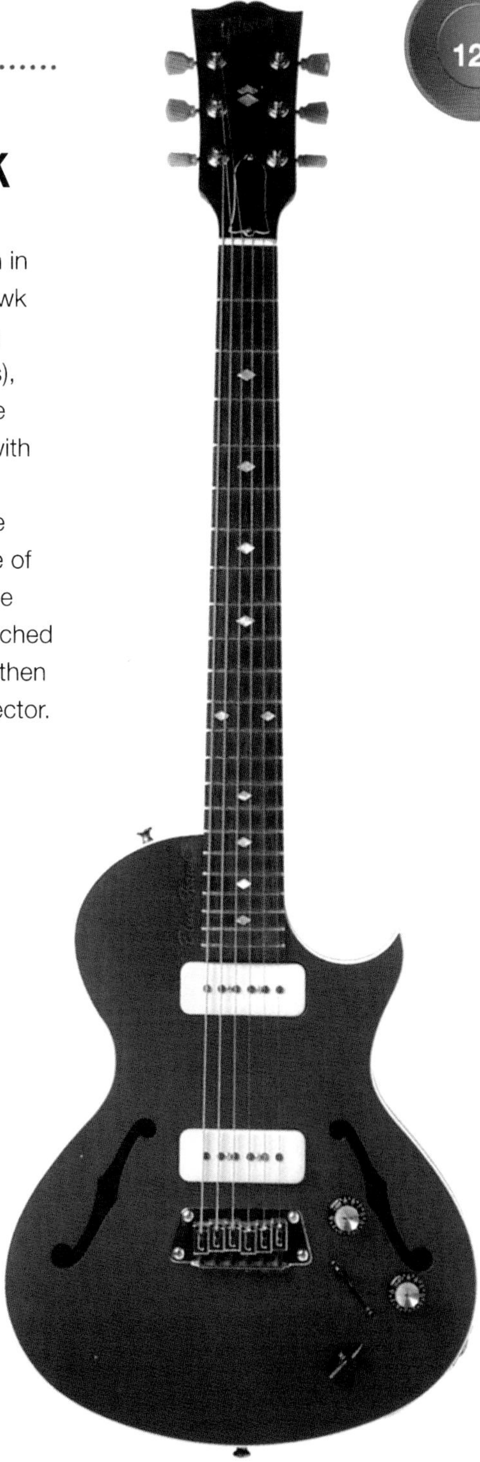

Gibson "Celebrity" Firebird

For many years, manufacturers have created "one-off" and limited edition instruments, in the hope that these will eventually attain the coveted status of a collector's item. Gibson's efforts in this are have been especially shrewd and successful. In 1988, the company's new management team launched a "Showcase" range of short-run guitars. In 1991, this was followed by the "Celebrity Series," which, like the "Showcase" category, was made up of familiar, but distinctively customized limited edition guitars. These were marked with a special decal, and supplied with a certificate of authenticity. With its black finish and gold hardware, this reverse-body Firebird is a "Celebrity."

The "Celebrity series" was made up of familiar models that were distinctively customized limited editions, and marked with this special decal.

Gibson Bob Marley Les Paul

Bob Marley (1945-1981) was the first reggae artist to attain international superstardom. He was often seen onstage with a heavily modified Gibson Les Paul Special. Specials had first appeared in 1955.

In 2002, Gibson's Custom, Art, and Heritage division produced a run of limited edition replicas of this instrument, one of which is shown here. Like many performers, Bob Marley customized his guitar. He replaced the original bridge/tailpiece with separate units, and substituted a aluminum pickguard for the factory-fitted black plastic one, adding a second piece of aluminum around the pickup selector switch on the guitar's upper bass bout. All these features were faithfully reproduced on the 2002 guitar.

Like many performers Bob Marley customized his instruments and this limited edition replica remains true to this with a rather homemade looking aluminum surround to the pickup selector switch.

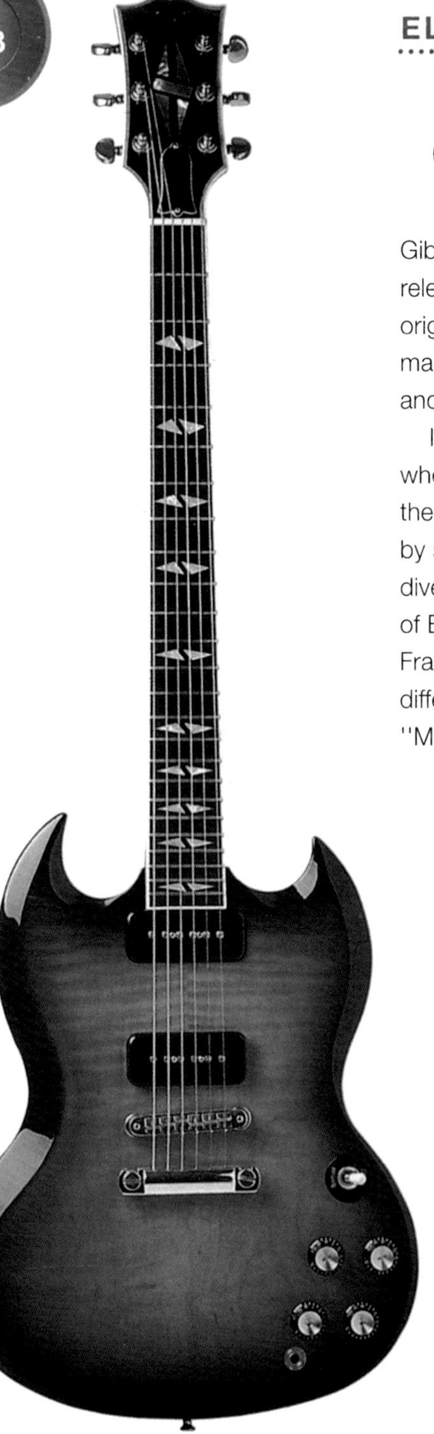

Gibson SG Supreme

Gibson launched the SG Supreme in early 1999. A press release described it as "a direct descendant of [Gibson's] original solid guitar, the Les Paul." With its maple-topped mahogany body, the instrument is certainly an elegant and fascinating hybrid.

It is also every bit as capable as its predecessors when it comes to delivering what Gibson describes as the instrument's "bad boy sound." This has been loved by several generations of rockers, including stars as diverse as Pete Townshend of The Who, Tony Iommi of Black Sabbath, Angus Young of AC/DC, and the late Frank Zappa. The SG is currently available in four different colors: "Lavaburst," "Emeraldburst," "Midnightburst," and "Trans Black."

The Supreme shown here is finished in "Fireburst" (a color no longer offered on this model) and has a gold-plated bridge and tailpiece.

Gibson L-00

The Gibson L-00 is believed to have debuted in 1925. Offered at a retail price of $25, it displaced the L-0 as Gibson's least expensive flat-top. Like the later L-0s, it measured 143⁄4 inches across, and had a mahogany back and sides, though it had a spruce top.

The L-00's emergence almost coincided with the Wall Street Crash. Its low cost and high quality helped Gibson to maintain production throughout the Great Depression, and the instrument had a particular appeal to bluesmen. In 1937, a more buoyant economic climate enabled Gibson to introduce a Hawaiian version of the guitar, named the HG-00. The L-00 itself was dropped at the end of World War II, but has recently been reissued.

Gibson Advanced Jumbo

In 1931, the first Martin-branded Dreadnought acoustics appeared. They were wider and more powerful sounding than any other flap-top guitar, and were soon attracting customers away from competitors. Gibson responded to the challenge by unveiling their "Jumbo" model in 1934. It had a characteristic "round-shouldered" look, and a 16-inch-wide mahogany body that provided reserves of volume quite sufficient to match its rivals. But its $60 price tag proved to be too high, and it was discontinued in 1930. The "Advanced Jumbo" was launched in the same year, priced at $80, but only remained available until 1940. It was reissued in the 1990s and gained recognition for the richness and subtlety of its tone.

This side-on detail shot shows the guitar's body, neck binding, and its immaculately finished frets.

Gibson SJ-200

By the later 1930s, Ray Whitley (1901-1979) was famous as a singer, and for his many "sidekick" roles in cowboy movies. He was also a successful songwriter, soon to make his name as the co-composer of "Back In the Saddle Again."

Fellow film cowboy Gene Autry was to adopt the song as his own. Gibson used Whitley to promote its latest acoustic guitar, a handsome jumbo, whose top was just less than 17 inches wide. It had a strikingly ornamented scratchplate, and a pearl-inlaid, mustache-shaped ebony bridge. The guitar was the first and most distinguished of the company's Super Jumbo range and went on the market in 1938. It sold for $200, and was therefore named the SJ-200.

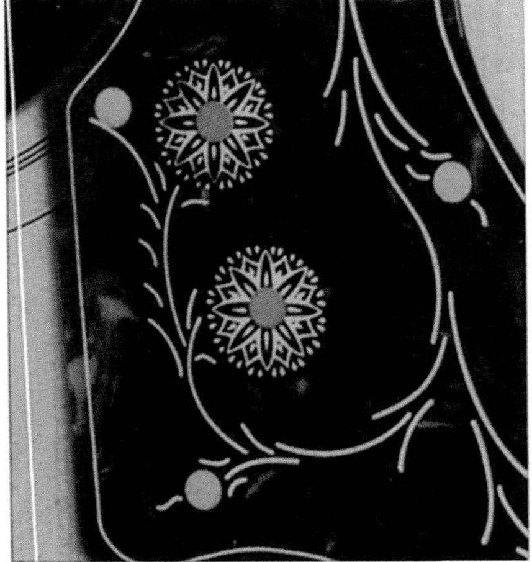

A detail of the strikingly ornamented scratchplate on the guitar that, in the 1940s, Gibson described as "the king of flat top guitars."

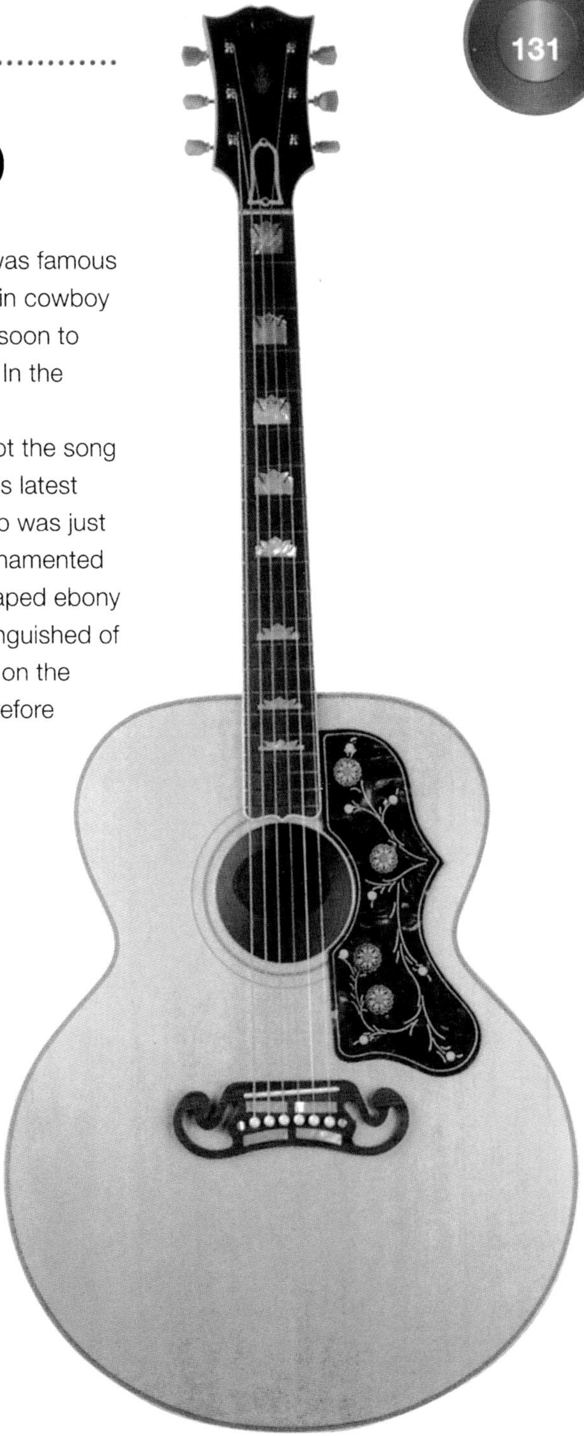

Gibson Southerner Jumbo

The saga of Gibson's Southerner Jumbo began (according to Gibson) when "a salesman for the southern territory brought home requests for a sturdy, versatile, and attractive round-should dreadnought." The first models to come out of Kalamazoo had rosewood backs and sides, but later SJs were made from mahogany (with spruce tops). Supplies of early SJs were limited by wartime restrictions, but the new guitar quickly attracted a following of prominent musicians. These included singer and political activist Woody Guthrie. Famously, Guthrie stuck a "This Machine Kills Fascists" label to the body of his Southerner. Discontinued in the late 70s, renamed "Southern Jumbos" are once more available.

The fingerboard is inlaid with pearl markers on this newly made version of the "Southern" Jumbo remains true to the original "Southerner" of the 1940s.

Gibson SJN Country Western

Gibson "Country-Western" flat-tops were simply Southerner Jumbos with natural finishes. The Country-Western name was retained only until 1960, when it was altered to SJN (Southerner Natural Jumbo). A more significant modification, which affected both the SJN and the original sunburst-finish Southerner Jumbo, was the replacement of their traditional bridges with adjustable saddles that could be raised or lowered by two screws. In 1962, the natural SJN received yet another new name, the SJN Country Western. Gibson extolled the model's "deep resonance, powerful tone, and deluxe appearance." A year later, the guitars received new, squarer body styling, similar to the Hummingbird.

A close-up view of the adjustable bridge first fitted to the SJNs in the early 1960s, but later replaced with a more conventional unit.

Gibson J-45

America's first full year of conflict in World War II was scarcely an auspicious time to launch new flat-top models. But in summer 1942, the company's latest acoustics, the J-45 and the Southerner, began shipping from its Michigan headquarters. Both were 16 inches wide, round-shouldered, spruce-topped jumbos that initially carried the motto "Only A Gibson Is Good Enough." The J-45's appearance was somewhat Spartan, but its gutsy tone quickly endeared it to customers. In spite of the uncertainties of wartime production, it went on to become a best seller. Post-1945, the J-45 succeeded in retaining its status as a popular "workhorse" instrument, despite several changes in design. This instrument is from 1969.

Gibson J-50

The Gibson J-50 shared the same basic specification as the J-45, but had a natural finish instead of the latter's normal sunburst one. It was officially introduced in 1947, but may have been available from 1942. Initially priced at $100 ($10 more than a J-45). The J-50 enjoyed a wide appeal, especially among folk, country and blues players.

One of the first major names to be associated with it was Tammy Wynette, who is said to have chosen it because its tone matched her singing style. Former Martin user, Bob Dylan, bought one in the early 1960s, and used it on his debut album, Bob Dylan, released in 1962. Current devotees include singer songwriters Elvis Costello and Gillian Welch.

Although this J-50 no longer has an adjustable bridge, this stamp fitted inside its body indicates that one was originally fitted to it.

Gibson Hummingbird

The first Hummingbird, launched in 1960, was the first of Gibson's square-shouldered acoustic guitars. It had an exquisite pickguard inlay, designed by staffer Hartford Synder. The company promoted the guitar as being the "big, round, and full...with the deep rumbly bass so prized by guitar players." It had been specially tailored for vocal accompaniment, and promised prospective buyers that the Hummingbird could be relied upon to provide a combination of "resonant tone, carrying power and striking beauty." The instrument lived up to expectations: folk and country pickers admired its mellow, rich timbre; pop and rock performers found it ideal for creating hard-driving rhythm.

The exquisite pickguard inlay designed by Gibson staffer Hartford Synder makes the Hummingbird the fanciest flat-top to come out of Kalamazoo since the late 1930s.

Gibson J-180 (Everly Brothers)

In the Everly Brothers early performing days, Don played a Gibson Southern Jumbo, his ''first brand-new guitar.'' Later, both Everlys were pictured with Gibson SJ-200s, which were soon embellished (by Gibson) with custom-made, oversized pickguards, cut to the brothers' own design. This was to become a key visual feature of Gibson's ''Everly Brothers'' jumbo, which was introduced in 1962. It also boasted star-shaped inlays on the headstock and fingerboard, and was finished in black. Everly models with natural tops were introduced in 1962. This new model was made at Gibson's factory in Bozeman, Montana. It undeniably performs better than its predecessor, but 1960s Everlys retain a special cachet.

The J-180 has a rosewood fingerboard and bridge. Its neck is maple, and its back and sides mahogany.

Gibson John Lennon J-160E 'Peace'

The Gibson J-160E was introduced in 1954. Featuring a discreetly positioned single-coil pickup. It was primarily aimed at players seeking both the practicality of an electric guitar and the conventional elegance of an acoustic jumbo. Originally aimed at country and western players, it found its greatest fame when John Lennon and George Harrison of The Beatles adopted it.

Both switched to standard electrics for most of their later work, but Lennon retained soft spot for his J-160E, replacing its original sunburst coloring with a psychedelic paint job in 1967, then giving it a natural finish prior to using it for his "Bed-In" peace protests with Yoko Ono in 1969. This guitar replicates the "Bed-In" version.

The discreetly positioned single-coil pickup gave the conventional appearance of an acoustic jumbo with the advantages of an amplified sound.

Gibson Country Gentleman

After the introduction of his nylon-strung acoustic by Gibson in 1982, Chet Atkins went on to collaborate with the company on updated versions of two instruments bearing his name that had first been produced by Gretsch in the late 1950s. One of these was the Country Gentleman, an electric archtop, which appeared in its new Gibson form in 1986.

The Gretsch Country Gentlemen were made between 1957 and 1972. The Gibson version of the guitar was given 335-style solid center block to improve its performance at higher volume levels, and to boost sustain. Other changes included the replacement of Gretsch's "Filter 'Tron" pickups with a pair of Gibson humbuckers and a banjo-type armrest.

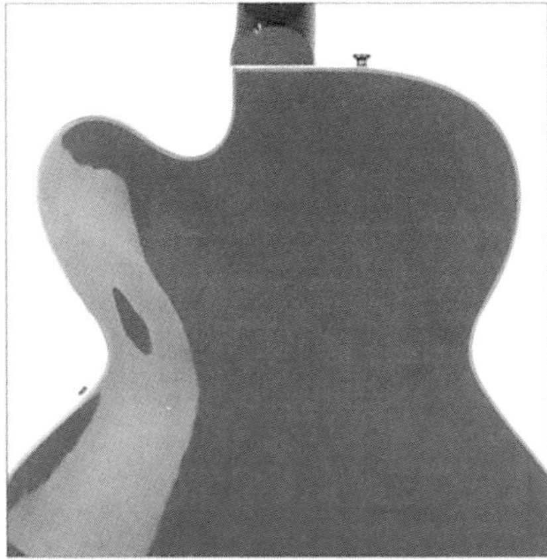

The contoured back of the Country Gentleman is made from maple and poplar laminate and finished in "Western Orange."

Gibson Chet Atkins CE

The classical electric (CE), an electric nylon-strung guitar with a solid body that would make feedback problems a thing of the past, represented the first fruits of the collaboration between Gibson and Chet Atkins. This relationship dated from the early 1980s. Chet had been searching for an effective electric classic for years, and had commissioned a prototype solid-body model from Kentucky-based luthier Hascal "Hack" Haile (1906-1986). This model was shown to Gibson, and served as the basis for the "CE" that the company introduced in 1982. The guitar in our photographs was made that same year. Unlike some later electric classics, the CE retains the look of its more traditional counterparts.

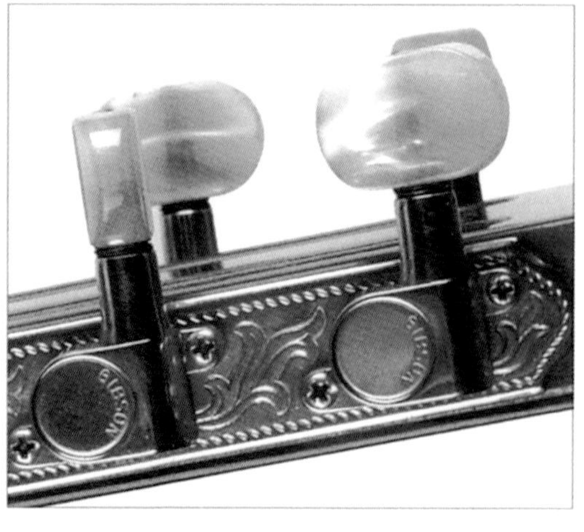

Both the CE and its wider-necked companion, the CEC, boast gold-plated, classical- style tuners specially made for Gibson by Schaller.

Dobro DM33 'Hawaiian'

In 1994, Gibson took over the Original Musical Instrument (OMI) firm, which had been manufacturing Dobros since 1967 under the direction of the Dopyera family. Today, OMI is part of Gibson's Original Acoustic Instrument division. This is based at the Gibson Bluegrass Showcase in the Opry Mills shopping mall near Nashville, Tennessee. Members of the publican watch models such as this DM33H Dobro being constructed, assembled, and finished. An extensive selection of other metal and wood-bodied acoustic and electric Dobros is also currently available from Gibson, including the popular reasonably priced Hound Dog model. As a result, the future of this classic resonator instrument seems secure.

The beautifully illustrated back of the DM33. Alternative designs available were the "Sailboat" and "California Girl" etchings.

Godin Multiac Steel Duet

Canadian designer and musician Robert Godin has been the driving force behind a number of successful and innovative acoustic brands, such as Art & Lutherie, and Norman. However, it is the product line bearing its own name, established in 1987, that features his most cutting-edge instruments, electrics and electro-acoustics. These instruments combine traditional craftsmanship and high technology in ingenious ways. Godin's Multiac series includes both nylon- and steel-strung models.

This Multiac is a steel duet. This instrument has a mahogany body with two acoustic chambers, but is intended to be heard through an amplifier or a PA system, and has two blendable transducers, hence "Duet."

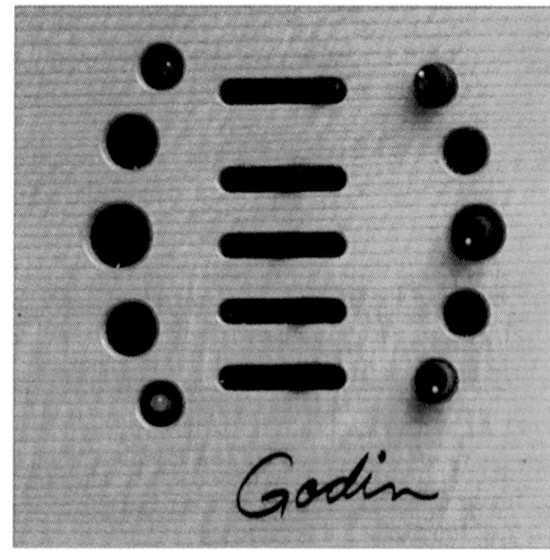

A detail of the Godin's knobs and slider controls, which adjust to blend the instrument's pickups.

Godin xtSA

The Godin xtSA offers players three separate ''voices,'' which can be deployed separately or combines. Its ''standard'' electric guitar tones are produced via three magnetic pickups: a single single-coil unit, and two humbuckers at the neck and bridge positions. For realistic ''acoustic guitar'' sounds, the xtSA has transducers imbedded in each of its bridge saddles. The xtSA's third output is a ''hexaphonic'' one, via which signals from each of the guitar's six strings can be used to trigger a synthesizer and create and create an almost unlimited range of sounds.

The xtSA's body is made from silver leaf maple and poplar. It has a mahogany neck and an ebony fingerboard. They are built in Berlin, New Hampshire.

The Godin's silver leaf maple body has four slider controls in the upper bass bout that adjust volume, treble, midrange and bass, levels on the transducers buried in the bridge saddles.

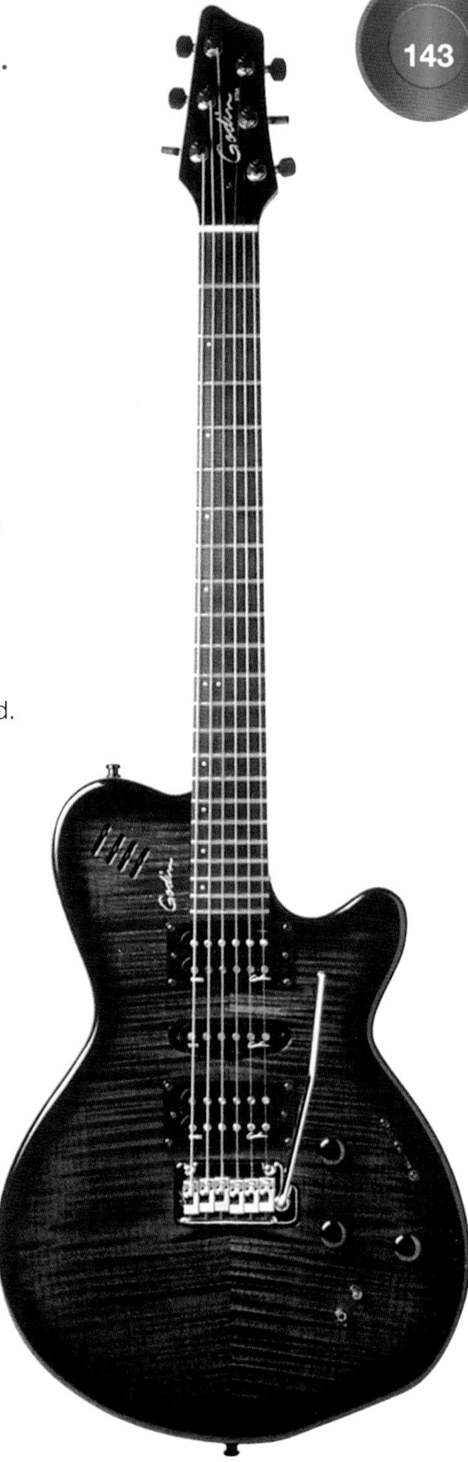

Gretsch 'Synchromatic'

The Fred Gretsch Company was set up in Brooklyn, New York, in 1883. Its founder, Friedrich Gretsch was a German immigrant. He died in 1895. The family firm was both a manufacturer and distributor.

Its first acoustic archtop guitars appeared in 1933, and six years later, it began using the ''Synchromatic'' name. Gretsch's ''Synchromatic'' acoustics were to retain a favored place in the company's catalogs for several years to come. The one shown here is a Super Auditorium model dating from 1952. Its features includes a slim, fast-playing ''Miracle Neck, ''a 16-inch top made from fine, straight grained spruce, and has a distinctively shaped ''stairstep'' bridge that dates from the 1930s.

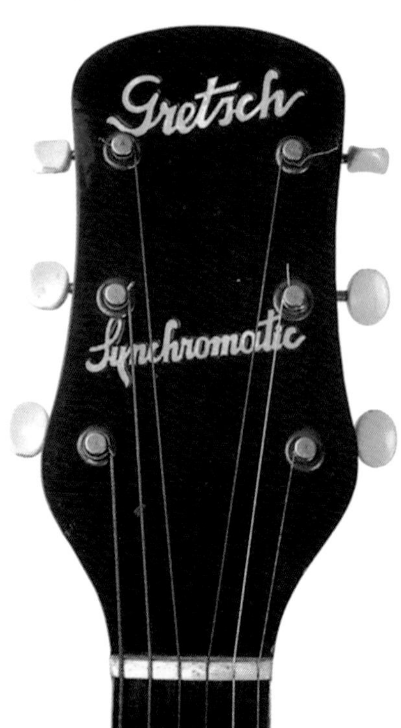

Gretsch Country Club

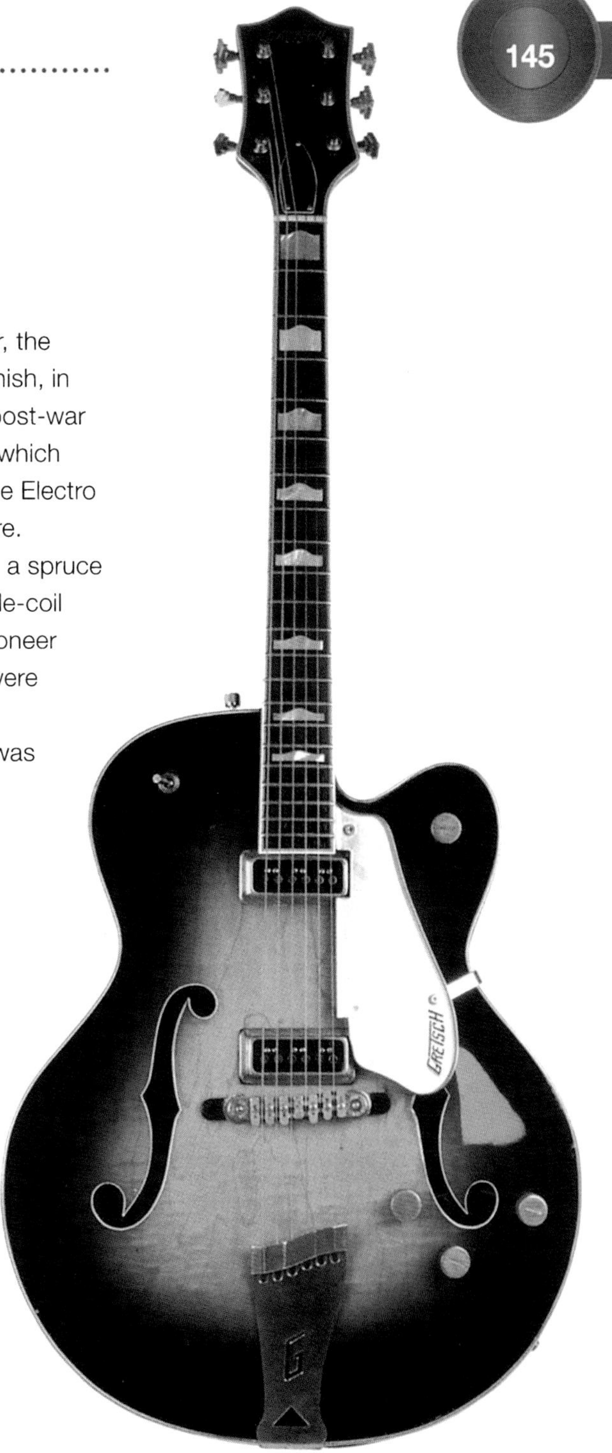

Gretsch launched its first archtop electric guitar, the single-pickup, maple-bodied Electromatic Spanish, in 1940. Gretsch enjoyed more success with its post-war electrics, and its popular Country Club model, which debuted in 1954, was an updated version of the Electro II, a model that had appeared three years before.

This Country Club was made in 1956. It had a spruce top and maple back and sides. It has twin single-coil pickups, "Dynasonics" invented by an early pioneer of transducer design, Harry DeArmond. They were manufactured in Toledo, Ohio. It is fitted with a "Melita" bridge, first introduced in 1952. This was the first such Gretsch unit to for allow precise adjustment.

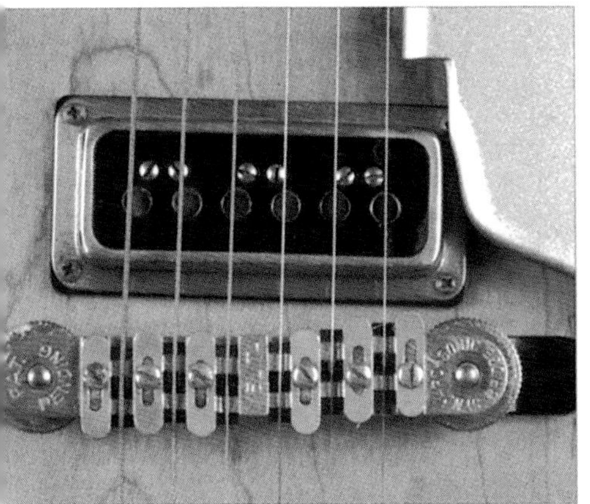

On this "Melita" bridge designed by Gretsch contractor, Sebastiano Melita, each string rests on its own adjustable bakelite saddle.

Gretsch 6121 Chet Atkins

By the mid-1950s, Chet Atkins (1924-2001) was already one of Nashville's most respected guitarists, with several best-selling records and many high-profile TV and radio appearances to his name. He became a Gretsch endorsee in 1954, and the company introduced two new electric models bearing his signature. These were the Chet Atkins Hollow Body (6120), and the Chet Atkins Solid Body (6121).

While these instruments are described in the firm's 1955 catalog as a ''blend of Chet Atkins' own ideas... with Gretsch 'know-how,' '' some aspects were not to the musician's liking, especially the Western-style decorations on their headstocks and fret markers, and the saddle-leather body binding on the 6121.

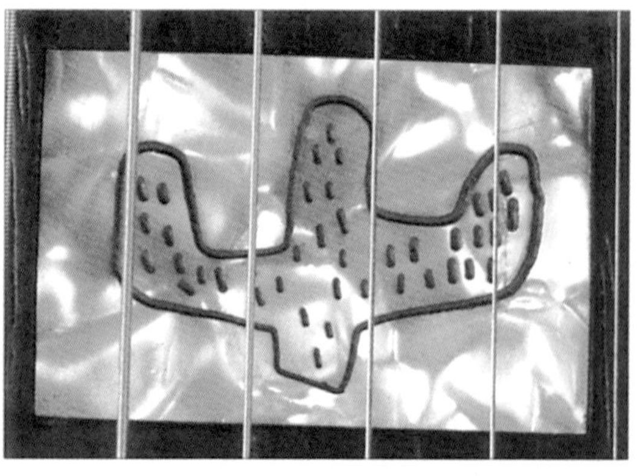

The western-style decorations like this cactus on the fret markers were not to Chet Atkins' personal taste however surviving examples like this one are highly prized by collectors.

Gretsch 6120 (Nashville)

The Gretsch 6120 Chet Atkins Hollow Body debuted in 1954, and, like the Solid Body 6121, the guitar initially featured Western-style decorations, and a large black "G" on its top. After Chet voiced his disapproval, such fripperies were quickly dropped from the 6120. This version, renamed Nashville, dates from 1967 and is comparatively staid in appearance. Over the years since it introduction, Gretsch had also made some modifications to the original 1954 design, and can be seen on this model. By this time, the DeArmond pickups fitted to earlier 6120s have been replaced by humbucking "Filter 'Trons." All 6120s made from 1961 onwards had a double cutaway, and painted-on f-holes. These resulted from Gretsch's decision to seal the top to reduce feedback.

The 6120's headstock was fitted with a sober-looking metal nameplate that was more to Chet Atkins's personal taste than the steer's head that appeared on the original Atkins Hollow Bodys.

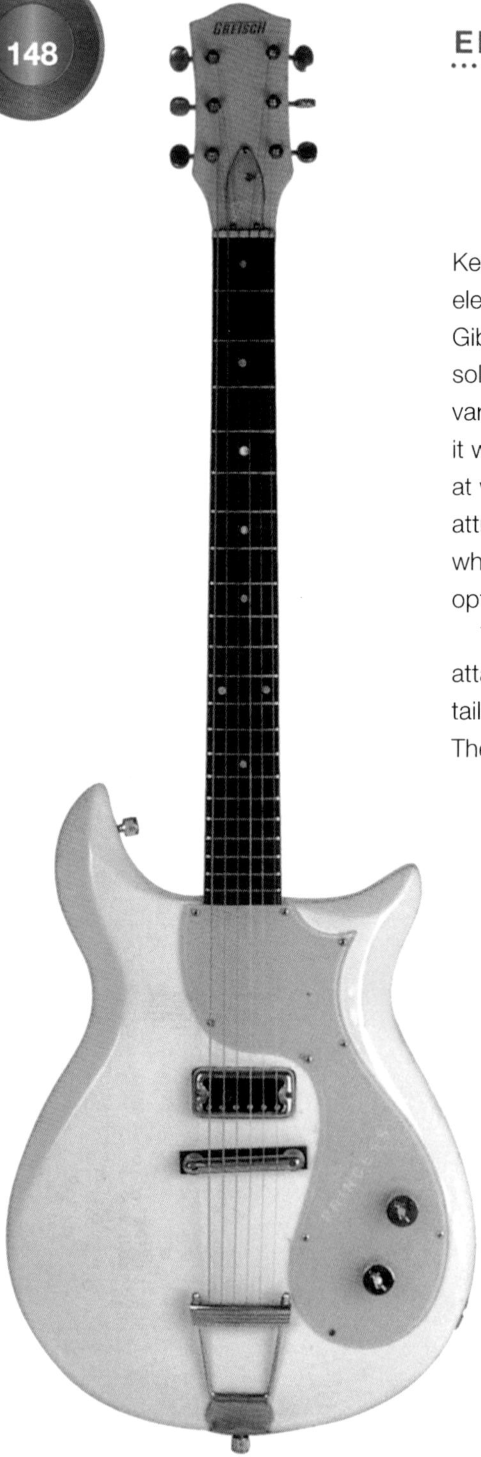

Gretsch Princess

Keen to capitalize on the growing market for solid-body electrics that was already being exploited by Fender and Gibson Gretsch introduced its double-cutaway Corvette solid in 1961. A year later, the firm unveiled a restyled variant of the Corvette, the Princess. Priced at $169, it was probably the first-ever electric specifically aimed at women players. Gretsch hoped that they would be attracted by the instrument's "feminine" color scheme, which included pink and white and blue and white options.

The Princess also had a "Tone Twister" that was attached to the strings between the bridge and the tailpiece, and was intended to provide a vibrato effect. The model was dropped in 1964.

The volume and tone controls on this Princess are not the original ones, and the instrument has also lost its "Tone Twister" palm vibrato.

Gretsch Elliot Easton Duo Jet

The 6128 Gretsch Duo Jet debuted in 1953. Though nominally a solid, it concealed a substantial degree of chambering beneath its mahogany top. This design quirk was discontinued in 1970, when the guitar became a true solid. It was acclaimed by Gretsch as having "solid tone projection, wonderful sustain, [and an] infinite variety of tonal coloring." The guitar's association with Beatle George Harrison ensured its survival until the early 70s. Gretsch itself was shut down in 1980, but re-emerged in 1989. Eleven years later, a Signature Jet model, endorsed by former Cars and Creedence Clearwater Revisited guitarist Elliot Easton, was announced. It has a slightly longer scale and "Filter 'Tron" pickups.

Elliot Easton of Creedence Clearwater Revisited endorsed the Signature Jet model and his signature appears on the guitar's pickguard.

Gretsch G6120 Brian Setzer

Brian Setzer shot to prominence in the 1980s with his trio, the Stray Cats. Since 1992, he has been serving up his distinctive brand of big band rockabilly with the Brian Setzer Orchestra.

A longtime fan of Gretschs, he purchased a 1959 "6120 Nashville" electric in New York in 1999, and had used it extensively onstage. Gretsch's "Artist Signature Model" range currently contains a pair of 6120-s closely resembling this prized guitar. Named the G6120SSU and G6120SSL, they have identical specifications, but slightly different finishes. This model is the SSL. Like other Setzer-endorsed instruments, they feature pickups designed by TV Jones, and "white dice" control knobs like those on Setzer's original Gretsch.

Using a dice as a volume control knob on the Setzer Gretsch was inspired by a line mentioning them in his song "Drive like Lightning (Crash Like Thunder)."

Gretsch Silver Falcon

This Japanese-made Silver Falcon is a direct descendant of the famous #6136 White Falcon. This was Gretsch's 1955 top-of-the-range model, priced at an astronomical $600. Featuring gold-plated hardware, sparkly inlays and "wing"-decorated fret markers, it was an extraordinarily glamorous guitar. Gretsch described it as "an instrument for the artist-player whose calibre justifies and demands the utmost in striking beauty, luxurious styling, and peak tonal performance, and who is willing to pay [for this]." The Falcon disappeared from production in the early 1980s, but was revived in 1990 and has subsequently been joined in the Gretsch catalog by Black (1992) and Silver (1995) Falcons.

The "sparkle" embellishments on the Falcon's "wings," Grestch logo, and truss-rod cover are not dissimilar to those seen on the company's drumkits.

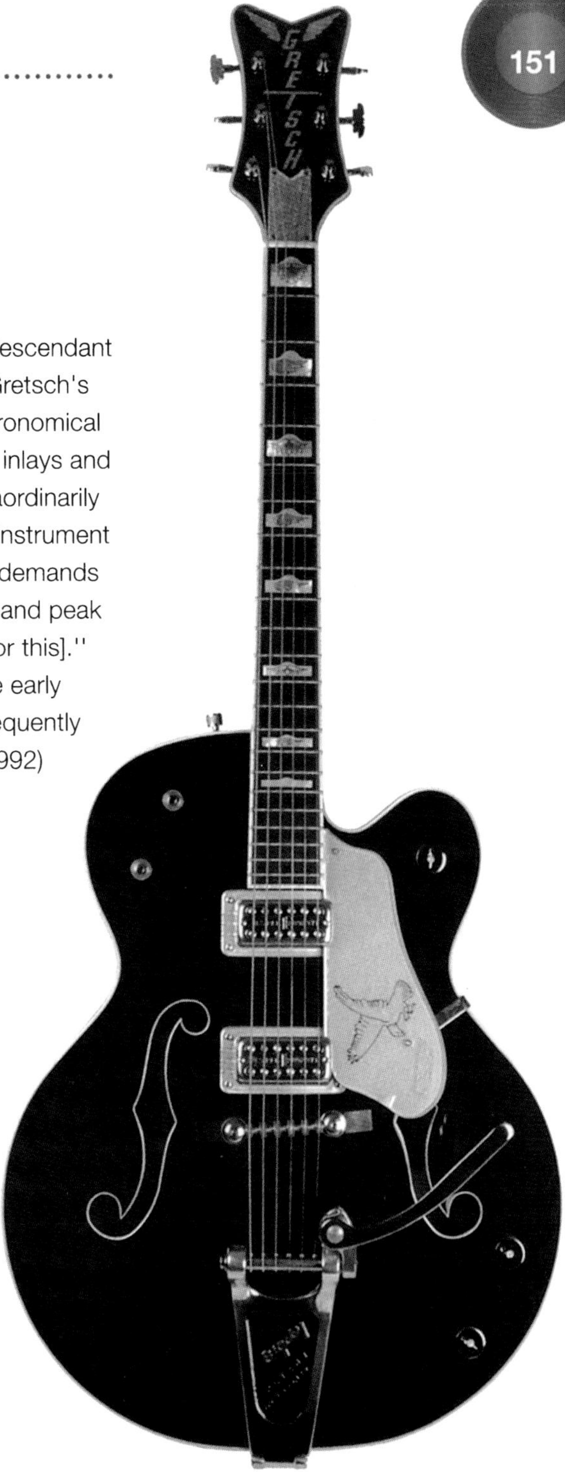

Guild Artist Award Archtop

The Guild Company was founded in New York in 1952 by Polish-born store proprietor and musician Alfred Dronge (1911-1972) and his business partner George Man. Mann had formerly worked for Epiphone, and soon established Guild's impressive reputation for its instruments. These were especially highly regarded by some of the Big Apple's leading jazz players. In 1955, one of this elite group, Johnny Smith, agreed to collaborate with Dronge on the development of a Guild archtop, to be named the Johnny Smith Artist Award.

The instrument appeared a year later. But due to a disagreement over its specifications, the musician never used it in public or in the studio. Smith's name was dropped in 1960.

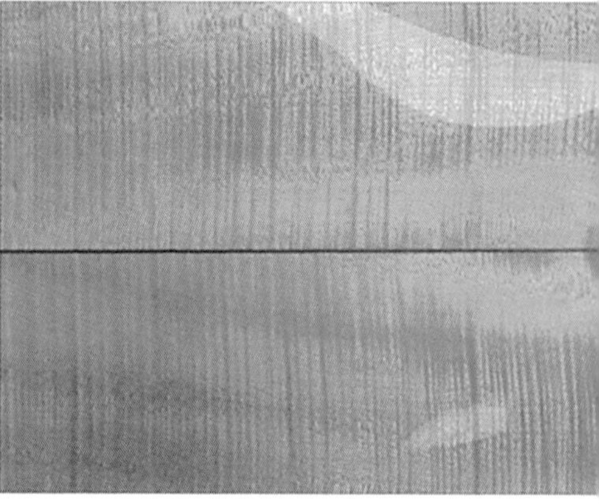

A close-up of the Guild Artist's beautifully figured maple laminated back which as the name suggests is truly a work of art.

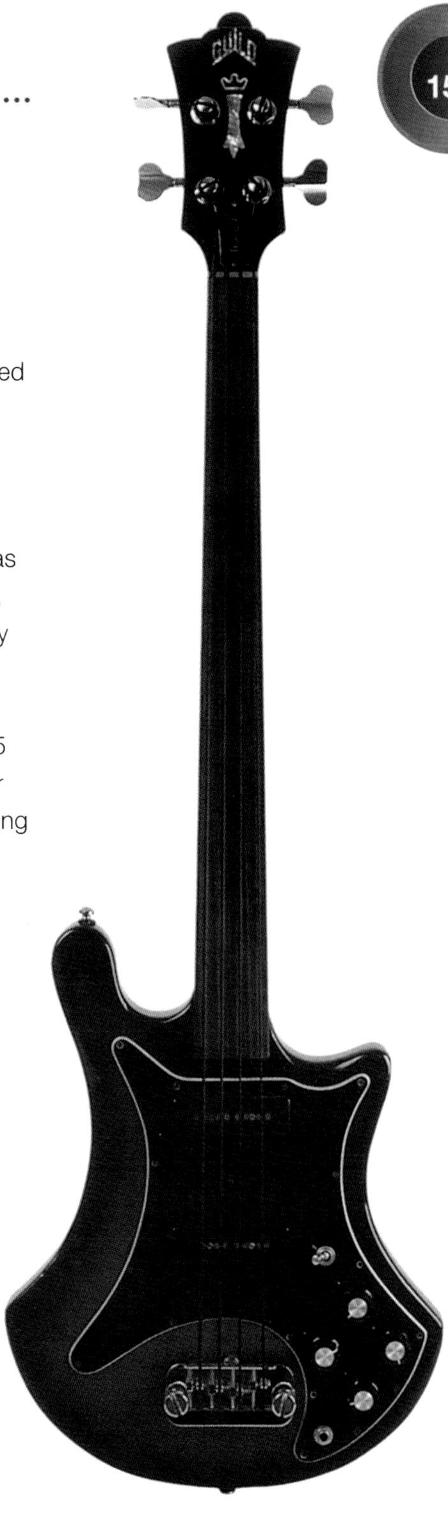

Guild B-302F Fretless Bass

Guild's first bass guitar, the solid-body Jet-Star, debuted in 1964. Like nearly all the company's basses, it was closely modeled on an existing 6-string design. In this case, the Thunderbird electric that had appeared the previous year. A Swedish company supplied its single pickup. 1965 saw the launch of the Starfire bass, It was quickly adopted by Jack Casady of Jefferson Airplane, who achieved a "beefy, resonant, and wonderfully dirty tone" with his customized Starfire.

Guild continued to produce distinctive basses throughout the late 1960s and 70s, including the M-85 (1967), the B-301 (1976), and B-302 (1977). With their long-scale fretboards, optional stereo wiring, and striking looks, the "Bs" sold steadily.

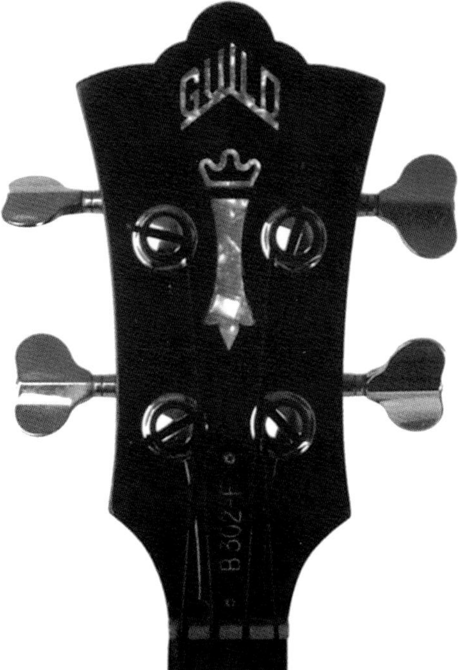

Guild F-112 12-String

1963 saw not only the launch of Guild's dreadnought range, but also, that December, the introduction of its first two 12-string flat-tops: the 16-inch F-212 and the slightly narrower F-312. In 1966, an even smaller companion, the 15½-inch wide F-112, which is shown here, joined these. Several other models followed. The new range, which in the tradition of Guild, was competitively priced, found its way into the hands of many up-and-coming performers. 12-string Guilds were soon a familiar sight at folk clubs and festivals. They were later to win even wider fame, thanks to their association with high-profile users such as singer-songwriter John Denver, Steve Miller, and Slash from Guns N' Roses.

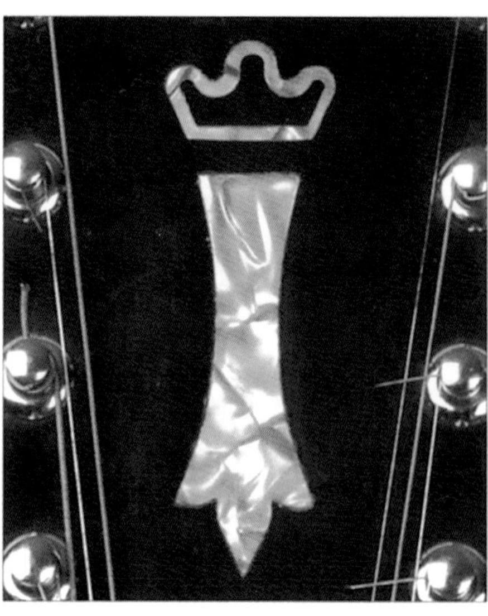

The Guild symbol inlaid into its headstock is known as a "Chesterfield," as it resembles the logo on a Chesterfield cigarette packet.

Guild T-100D

Guild's electric models, like its acoustics, sometime had names with a faintly exotic, European flavor. Its mid-1950s archtops included the Granada and Capri, both were 16⅜ inches wide, and just under 3 inches deep. But when Guild introduced a shallower version of the Capri in 1958, it chose a more informal label, the ''Slim Jim.'' The instrument was described as ''light in weight and easy to handle.''

Two versions were available. T-100 had a single pickup, while the T-100D had two transducers and a fancier, ''harp''-style tailpiece. Both models had a Florentine cutaway, and were made from laminated maple. The T-100D has been described as having ''that lovely Rockabilly sound'' of the 50s.

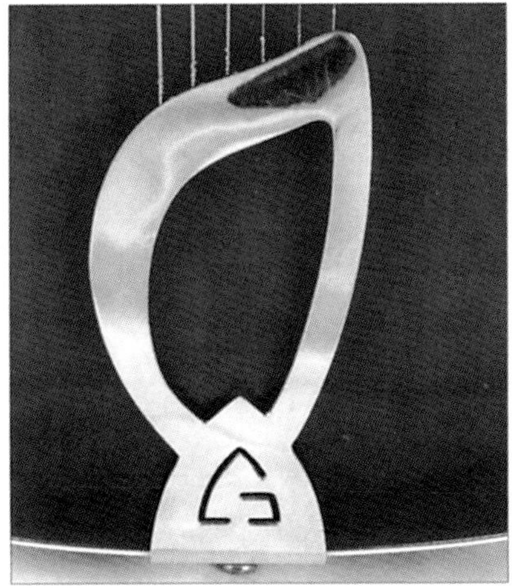

The fancy ''harp''-style tailpiece was available on the two-transducer T-100D. The cheaper T-100 model had only a single pickup.

Guild X-175

The X-175 "Manhattan" was one of Guild's earliest instruments. A companion to the one-pickup X-150 "Savoy," the Manhattan had a spruce top, with maple back and sides, and was initially fitted with two single-coil transducers.

These were later replaced with humbuckers. The guitar was aimed principally at the jazz musicians who were Guild's earliest supporters. In its original form, the guitar had some similarities to 1940s and 50s Epiphones, and many Guild employees had worked for that company. It was designed to provide "professional tone quality [and] distortion free performance," but it can also supply a rich, fruity timbre ideal for rock and blues. This X-175 was made in the early 1980s.

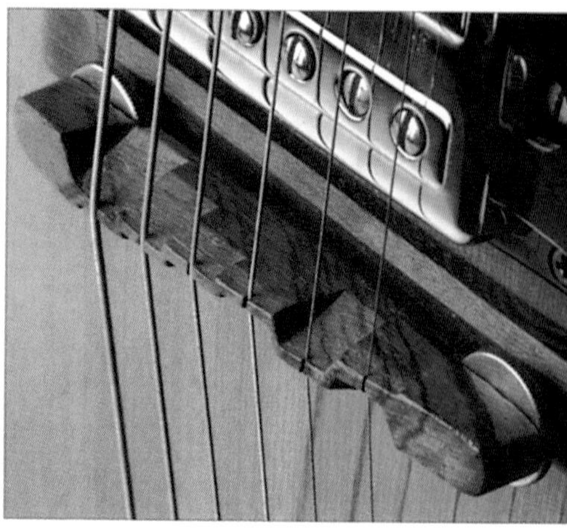

This wooden bridge is adjustable for height, but, unlike more sophisticated units, has only preset positions for individual string intonation.

Guild X-170

Although the original X-175 Manhattan was dropped from the Guild catalog in 1984 after two decades in production, the company soon introduced a substitute for it. Named the X-170 "Mini-Manhattan," it was slightly narrower and thinner than its distinguished predecessor. With its internal soundpost, and more rigid, laminated maple top was better able to resist feedback in noisy onstage conditions.

The guitar was also given a glamorous new look, with gold plating on its pickups, machine heads, and "harp" tailpiece. But times were hard for Guild in the 1980s, and the company saw two changes of ownership. In 1995, Fender purchased Guild. It is now based alongside its parent in Corona, California.

Harmony Rocket III

Harmony, founded in Chicago in 1892, became a major supplier of inexpensive stringed instruments to retailers and catalog houses, including Sears, Roebuck & Company, which purchased it in 1916. A subsequent endorsement deal with vaudeville, movie and radio star Roy Smeck, who excelled on guitar, banjo, and ukulele, bought Harmony even greater prosperity.

In the post-war era it skillfully adjusted its product range to match new musical trends by offering attractive, if basic, electrics alongside its longer-established lines. The Harmony Rocket range of electric guitars debuted in 1958. The name seems to have been chosen in response to the "space-age" overtones of Fender's Stratocaster.

Despite being a cut-price model, this 1962 Harmony Rocket III is a nicely finished instrument with three pickups, a single cutaway and an ultra-thin body.

Harmony H22 Bass

Harmony's H22 ''Hi-Value'' electric bass is often referred to as a ''Rocket'' bass, perhaps it sometimes shared a catalog page with the company's Rocket 6-strings. Introduced in 1961, it had a cutaway body, white pickguard, and a wooden finger rest (both of these have been removed from this example). It was fitted with a single pickup, designed, like those on the Rockets, in conjunction with DeArmond.

The white switch above its volume control altered the tonal response of its electronics, giving a choice of ''full bass'' or ''lighter baritone registers.'' It remained in production until 1968. The H22 is especially associated with British musician Ronnie Lane of the British group the Small Faces.

The H22's ''Torque-Lok'' neck is bolted to its laminated maple body.

Heritage H-550

When, in 1984, Gibson left its base in Kalamazoo, Michigan, having built guitars there for the previous 67 years. It seemed as though the town's great tradition of lutherie might be ending. But the Gibson factory was almost immediately taken over by a brand new firm, Heritage Guitars. Its co-founders were ex-Gibson employees, and its staff was mainly former Gibson craftsmen. Heritage's first instrument, a solid-body electric guitar, debuted in 1985.

Since then, the company has won numerous plaudits for the superb quality of its instruments. The Heritage H-550 was a full-depth semi-acoustic, perfect for jazz and blues. It boasts a maple body, two humbucking pickups, and mother-of-pearl inlays and bindings.

The laminated curly maple used for the H-550's top and body (and as a veneer on its pickguard) gives the instrument an elegant, sophisticated look.

Höfner 500/1 Bass

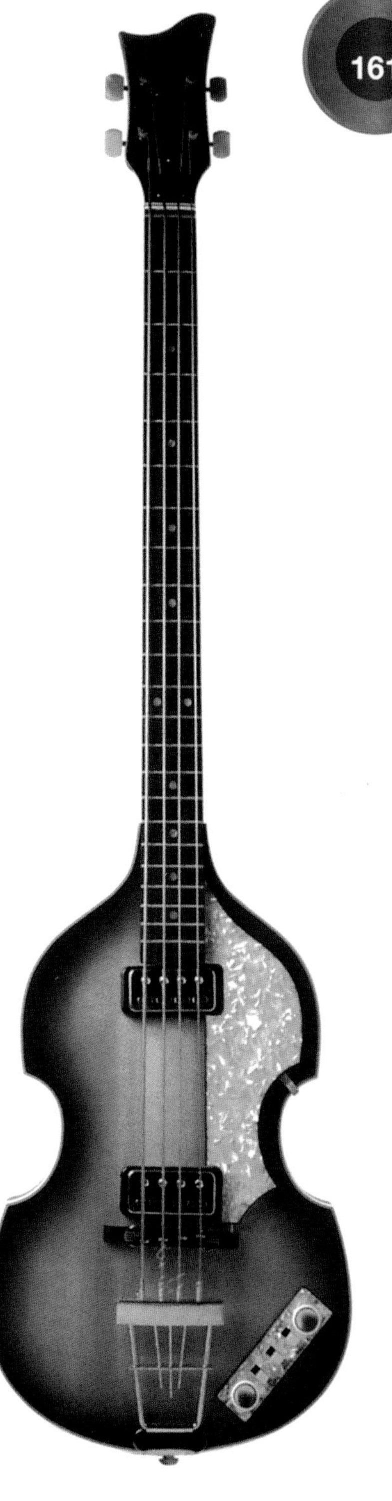

The Höfner 500/1 bass was the brainchild of Walter Höfner, son of the firm's founder, Karl. Its shape betrays Walter's background as a violinmaker, and its relatively small, hollow body gives it a pleasingly lightweight fee very different from most modern bass guitars. The 500/1 first appeared in Germany in 1956.

The little bass's most famous player, Paul McCartney, acquired his 500/1 in Hamburg, in the early days of the Beatles. McCartney revealed that, for him, one of its principal selling points was its symmetrical outline, which allowed him to play it left-handed without it "looking quite as stupid as some other [instruments] did." He didn't have a formal deal with Höfner, but every 500/1 bore his face and signature.

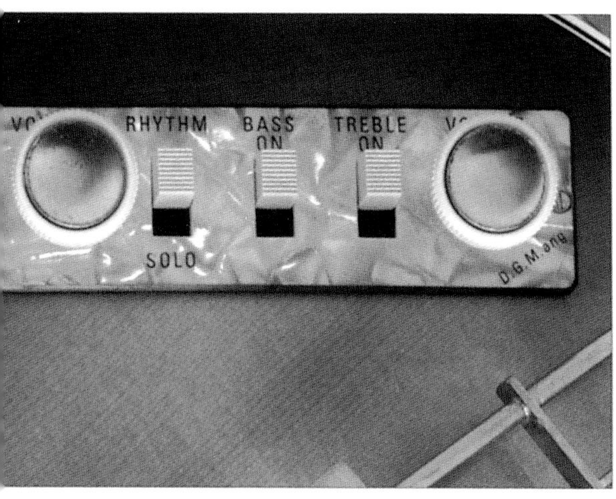

Despite its lack of tone controls, the 500/1 can produce a surprising range of timbres, although the pickup switching takes a little getting used to.

Höfner 172 Solid Body

By the early 1960s, the traditional, violin-inspired appearance of Höfner's archtops was beginning to seem dated, especially in comparison with Fender's slim, solid-bodied electrics. The German company responded by introducing its own solid guitars.

This 172 dates from around 1963. This model has only two pickups, but other 172s had three. It clearly shows the influence of the Fender stratocaster. It controls are basic and its finish relatively plain. Later Höfner solids were equipped with additional circuits and switches. By 1968, some were even sporting ostentatious colored vinyl body coverings. These instruments all sold well, though it is likely that many of their customers bought them because they were affordable.

The chunky pickup switch on the 172 is built to withstand years of rough treatment.

Hohner B24 Bass

Mattias Hohner in Trossingen, founded the Hohner Company, south of the German city of Stuttgart, in 1857. Its first product was the harmonica (invented in 1821), and accordions. In the 1960s, the company produced its own version of Ned Steinberger's revolutionary headless bass guitar, patented by him in 1980. These proved highly successful.

They were well made, and substantially cheaper than the graphite originals. Hohner was soon augmenting its headless range with a fretless bass and a five-stringer. It has continued to produce high quality Steinberger-licensed instruments. Its current catalog contains no less than four of these: three basses, and a 6-string guitar with a locking tremolo.

Ned Steinberger's brilliant concept of moving the tuners to the bridge end to produce the first headless bass was licensed to Hohner. His company, Steinberger Sound, is now part of Gibson.

Ibanez JTK1BT Jet King

The Hoshino Gakki Company started manufacturing musical instruments in the Japanese city of Nagoya in the 1930s. Thanks to a distribution deal with Harry Rosenbloom, a music store proprietor from Ardmore, Pennsylvania, their guitars began to appear in the USA in the 60s.

They were issued under the brand name "Ibanez." Initially, many of these instruments resembled classic Gibsons, Fenders, and Rickenbackers. But by the late 1970s, the company was developing instruments for leading American artists such as Bob Weir of the Grateful Dead, and George Benson. Their current catalog is impressively diverse. The Jet King range is for players who prefer a "retro" feel to their guitar.

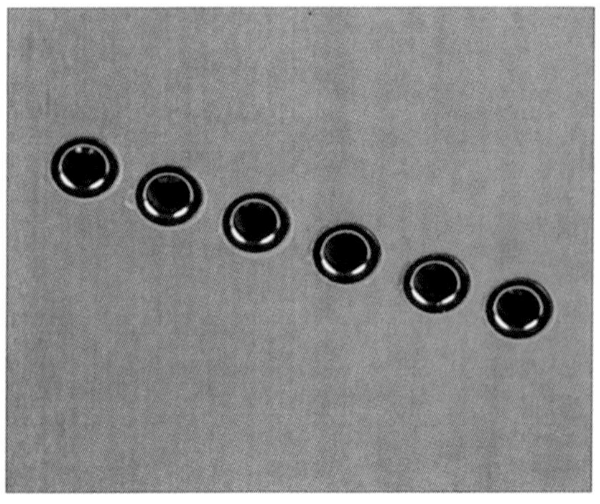

The JTK1's strings pass through its basswood body to maximize sustain.

Ibanez RG2620-CBL

Since they debuted in 1987, Ibanez's RG (Rock Guitar) electrics have been the ''weapon of choice'' for musicians seeking to ''visit sonic mayhem on the metal masses.'' The RGs' many fans include high profile players like Terry Balsamo of Evanescence. A number of RGs, including the RG 2620 featured here, are equipped with Edge Pro tremolos, whose sliding strike holders (which move when the unit's ''whammy bar'' is operated) are built into the main bridge assembly for maximum stability and sustain.

The 2620's striking looks complement its high performance, and its ''cubed pewter'' finish (available in blue or black) is hand-stamped onto its double-cutaway, basswood body.

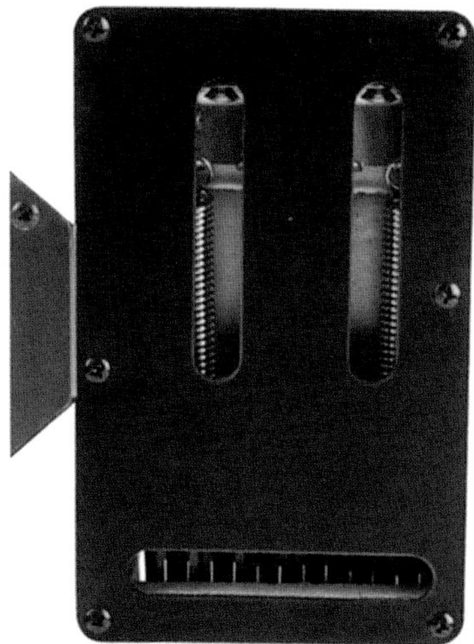

This rear view of the RG2620 shows part of the mechanism for its Edge Pro vibrato.

Ibanez GB10 George Benson

Many years before he achieved success as a pop singer, George Benson (b. 1943) had already been recognized as one of the finest jazz guitarists of his generation. For his recordings, Benson plays archtop Gibsons, but found these instruments had a tendency to feed back at high sound levels during live appearances.

Before long, he was in discussions with Ibanez over the development of a new electric guitar, tailor-made to his requirements, and bearing his name. The result was the Ibanez GB10, a 21/2 inch deep hollow-body, which was launched at the National Association of Music Merchants Association (NAMM) trade show in Chicago in 1977, and has remained in production ever since.

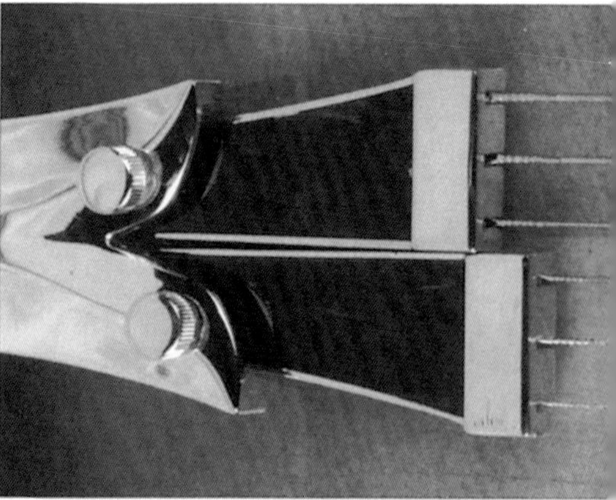

This handsome tailpiece (covered with gold like the rest of the GB10's hardware) features twin knobs that vary the tension of the upper and lower groups of strings.

Ibanez JEM555

Guitarist Steve Vai was born in 1960, and first came to prominence as a member of Frank Zappa's band in the early 1980s. He achieved wider fame with his work with David Lee Roth and Whitesnake, and is now a major name in his own right. Unlike many virtuosos, Vai does not favor vintage instruments, or ''classic'' Gibson and Fender designs. Instead, he had developed his own ''JEM'' range of electrics with Ibanez. The first of these were the three JEM777s launched in 1987. The company described these instruments as ''unique in form and function.'' They incorporated DiMarzio pickups and ultra-fast necks, and a ''monkey grip'' handle hollowed out of their bodies. The JEM555 debuted in 1994.

The famous JEM ''monkey grip'' machined into the basswood body both saves weight and makes the instrument easy to carry.

Jackson KVX10 King V

Wayne Charvel set up Charvel's Guitar Repair in southern California in 1974. His shop undertook refinishing work for Fender, while catering to the needs of rock star clients such as The Who, Deep Purple, and Eddie Van Halen. In 1978, Wayne Charvel sold his business to a member of his staff, Grover Jackson, who continued to trade under the Charvel name. He worked with many stars, including Ozzy Osbourne band member Randy Rhoads, and built a "Flying V"-like electric to his specification in 1980. Jackson was reluctant to use the Charvel name on this wild-looking axe, and signed his own last name on the headstock. The first Jackson guitar was born. This is the current production model, the KVX10.

Jackson DK2 Dinky

One of Jackson's most popular design categories is the so-called "Superstrat." The first production Superstrat named the Soloist, was launched in 1983-4. It featured a "neck-through-body" configuration, rather than the Fender-type bolt-on neck. It was soon joined by the Dinky, a "bolt-on" Superstrat that was otherwise very similar to its "neck-thru" cousin. Both are now recognized as Jackson classics.

The 2005 DK2 Dinky in our pictures remains faithful to the Superstrat tradition. The company's custom department has long been renowned for its ability to produce "anything from life-like figures to off-the-wall abstract concoctions." Grover Jackson left Jackson in 1989, which is now owned by Fender.

This Dinky has an alder body and a maple bolt-on neck; it boasts two Seymour Duncan humbucking pickups, a rosewood fingerboard, and shark fin inlays.

Kay Value Leader

Kay has been manufacturing musical instruments for both students and professional musicians since 1890, in its various incarnations. The company got its name from Henry Kuhrmeyer (1894-1956), whose nickname was "Kay." Kuhrmeyer and his wife moved to Chicago in 1920, and invested in the Stromberg-Voisinet Instrument Company. He attracted several talented luthiers to the company, and it thrived.

He gradually assumed control of Stromberg-Voisinet, and it became the Kay Musical Company in 1935. Sidney Katz bought Kuhrmeyer out in 1955. At this time, Kay's ambition was to dominate the "value" market, and the Value Leader range spearheaded this. Jazzman Lonnie Johnson played the instrument.

The Kay Value Leader parallelogram pickguard always had a slightly "homemade" look to it as did the controls and bridge.

Lakland Skyline Joe Osborn Bass

In 1994, Dan Lakin began manufacturing bass guitars in partnership with instrument technician Hugh McFarland. They christened the business Lakland. The company manufactured meticulously crafted basses started to attract leading players including the late Rick Danko, formerly of The Band. More recent customers have included US's Adam Clayton, Booker T, and the MGs and Blues Brothers stalwart Donald "Duck" Dunn, and Daryl Jones, who plays with the Rolling Stones. Today, Lakland is based in Chicago's Goose Island.

The Lakland model is shown here is a Skyline Joe Osborn is a celebrated session player. It represents a Fender Jazz bass, but incorporates updated pickups and other updates.

This neat bridge design allows the strings to pass either through the body (as here) or through the unit itself.

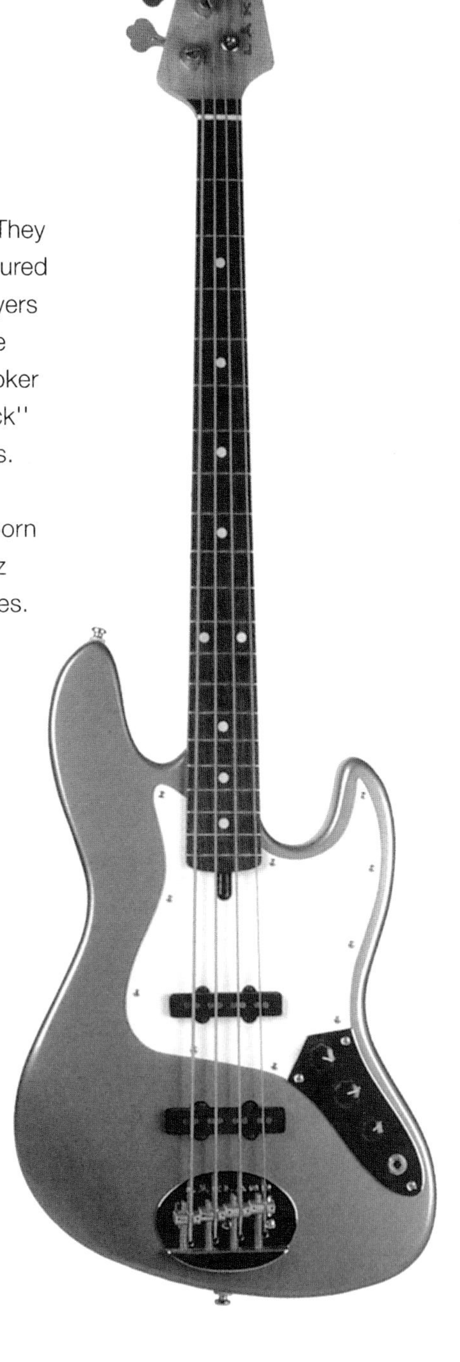

Line 6 Variax 700

Line 6, based in Agoura Hills, west of Los Angeles, is renowned for its pioneering work in developing digital devices that provide realistic recreations of classic amplifier sounds and effects. In 2003, it made a significant addition to its range of so-called "modeling" products when it launched the Variax, the first-ever guitar to offer simulations of a variety of instruments, from acoustic flat-tops to solid electrics, at the touch of a switch, offering what Line 6 describes as "the sounds of an entire guitar collection."

Reviewers gave the revolutionary new axe a warm reception. The featured model is a tremolo-equipped instrument from the company's 700 series, finished in translucent "Amber."

The right hand socket connects the Variax to standard amplifiers; the one on the left interfaces with other Line 6 modeling equipment, and can be used to transfer the guitars' sounds to a computer for editing.

Martin 0-28K

In Nazareth, Pennsylvania, C.F. Martin's guitar business flourished, he was obliged to adapt his elaborate European designs "to a rougher-edged, simpler American society" by making them "plainer [and] more utilitarian." Gradually, Martins lost their scrolled headstocks and abalone body inlays, and started to acquire outlines closer to those of a 20th century flat-top instruments. This 1927 guitar seen here is 131⁄2 inches wide, and while a "Style 28" like this one would normally have a rosewood back and sides, the K suffix indicates that koa has been used. The 0-28K's steel strings were, at the time of its introduction, a comparative novelty. Steel strings had replaced gut as standard on Martins in 1922.

Martin 0-15, 1942

At the time of their introduction in 1854, Martin "size 0" guitars, with a maximum body width of 131/2 inches, were the company's largest models. They remained so until the advent of the slightly larger "00" in 1877, but eventually came to be seen as relatively small instruments, following the introduction of the OMs and Ds in the 1930s. Inevitably, the 0s' modest dimensions restricted their ability to produce a big sound, but their sweet timbre and comfortable feel kept them in steady demand, especially among singers.

The company's new mahogany guitar, the 0-15 was launched in 1940. This was a Spartan-looking flap-top, but it sold well, and remained available until the early 1960s. This example dates from 1942.

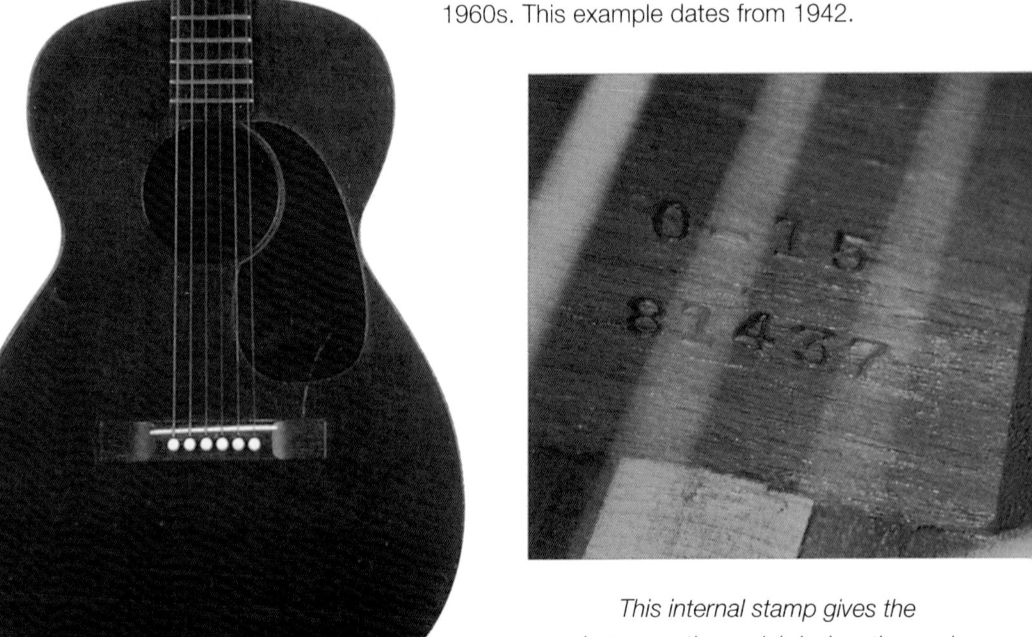

This internal stamp gives the instrument's model designation and individual serial number.

Martin 000-18, 1948

The Martin 000-18 debuted, in its original gut-strung version, in 1911. But came into its own in the 1930s and 40s, by which time it was sporting steel springs and a neck with 14 frets to the body, as does this 1948 example. Thanks to it 15-inch body width, it delivered a good deal more volume than smaller Martin flat-tops such as the 0-15. Its famous users included singer, writer, and political activist Woody Guthrie (1912-1967), and influential folk-style picker and vocalist Elizabeth Cotten (1895-1987). Elvis Presley also briefly owned a 000-18 in the mid-1950s (he later switched to a Martin D-18 Dreadnought), and among the instrument's current devotees is Martin Carthy, one of the UK's leading folk singers.

Martin Tenor, c.1926

Although the first C.F. Martin was trained as a luthier and violinmaker in Europe, Martin family tradition has it that he made no violins after his arrival in the USA in 1833. The Martin factory devoted itself solely to guitars until about 1895, when they began to manufacture a successful range of mandolins.

The company subsequently introduced ukuleles (in 1916), South American-style tiples (in 1919), and tenor guitars (in 1926). Instruments like this were tuned identically to a tenor banjo. They were initially popular with Dixieland jazzmen. Later, in the 1950s and 60s, they were taken up by folk performers such as Nick Reynolds of the Kingston Trio. Briefly reissued in 1997, Martin tenor guitars are no longer in production.

Martin 000C-16GTE

Opinions are divided over the best way of amplifying high-end flat-tops such as Martins. All existing solutions had their advantages and drawbacks, until Martin's introduction of the 000C-16GTE. This ingenuous instrument is fitted with a Fisherman Prefix Premium preamp system that can blend together (or select separately) the outputs of an under-saddle transducer and an internally mounted microphone.

The instrument's outstanding unamplified sound is worth taking the trouble to preserve. Its spruce top and mahogany body deliver all the mellow sweetness traditionally associated with 000 Martins, and its cutaway and Micarta (ebony substitute) fingerboard make it easy as well as rewarding to play.

The Martin Guitar company label glimpsed through the sound hole, inside the body, provides proof of the instrument's validity.

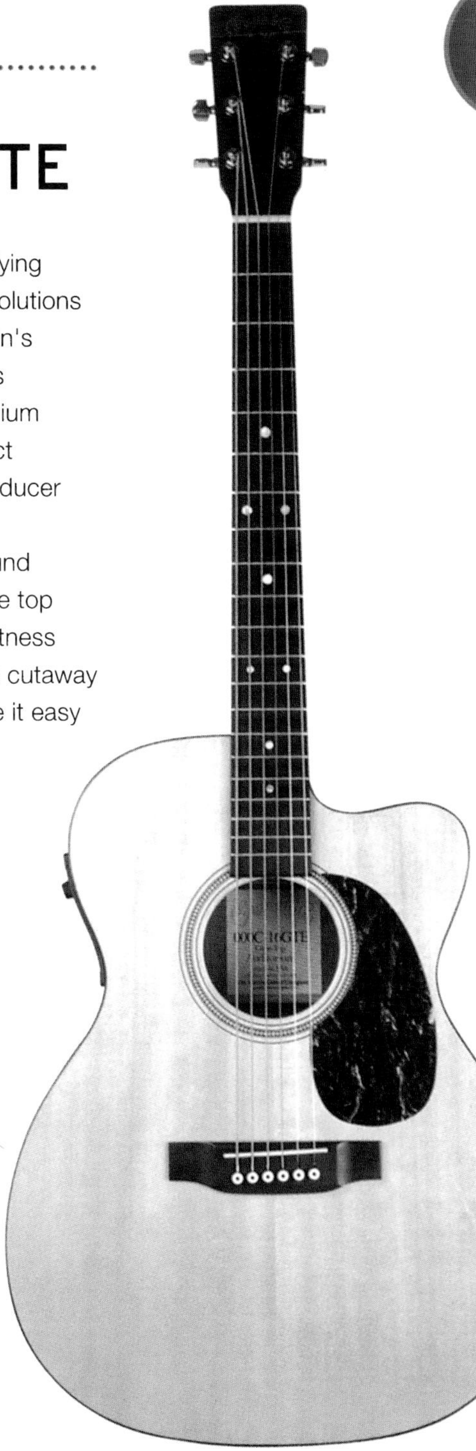

Martin D-18

The Oliver Ditson company had its origins in a music publishing business started by a Boston bookstore, Batelle's, in 1783. Later, the business expanded into selling instruments and ''Everything in Music and Musical Merchandise.''

In 1916, the company commissioned Martin to produce a line of Ditson-branded guitars, including a model with a body wider than Martin had ever produced. Martin supplied Dilson until 1921, and again between 1923 and 1930. After they were finally discontinued, Martin decided to continue with the large Ditson guitar, and created a new size category, ''D.'' This stood for ''Dreadnought,'' a name borrowed from the British navy vessel HMS Dreadnought.

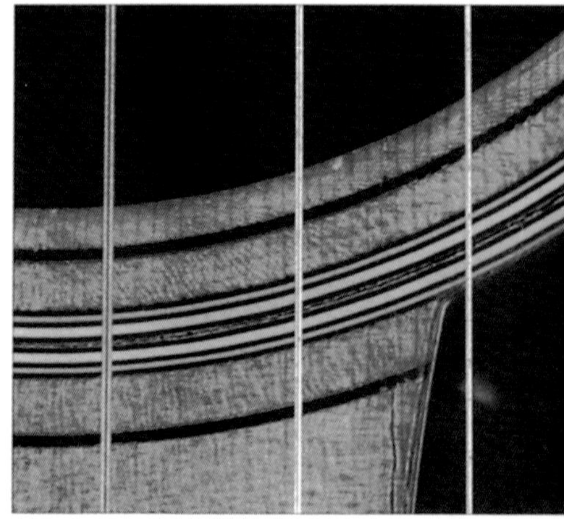

The sound hole of the D-18 contains multiple layers of contrasting binding let into the honey-colored spruce of the body.

Martin HD-28

Guitars produced in Martin's Style 28 incorporate an especially famous feature: the "herringbone" marquetry that embellishes their tops. First used in the 19th century, the herringbone trim is made from strips of intricately cut wood. This was originally bought in from European suppliers, but was later sourced domestically. The first Style 28 Dreadnoughts appeared in the early 1930s. They and the other "28s" continued to include herringbone decoration until 1946, when it was dropped. The lack of herringbone was a major disappointment to customers, and in 1976, Martin reintroduced it as a key feature of a new "Herringbone Dreadnought" category. The HD-28 was the first model to sport the revived trim.

Martin OMC-16E

Like the 000C-16GTE, this 21st century version of Martin's classic Orchestra Model features a high-specification Fishman preamp system, utilizing both a gooseneck-mounted microphone and a bridge-saddle pickup. But while the 000C-16 sports a conventional preamp panel on its side, the OM's remarkable unobtrusive "Ellipse" unit is positioned beneath the instrument's top, and its blend, volume, phase, and microphone trim controls are all accessible via the soundhole. The guitar itself is available with three different body woods. This example has a back and sides of figured koa. Maple and sapele are substituted for this on other OMC-16Es, although all the models have a Sitka spruce top.

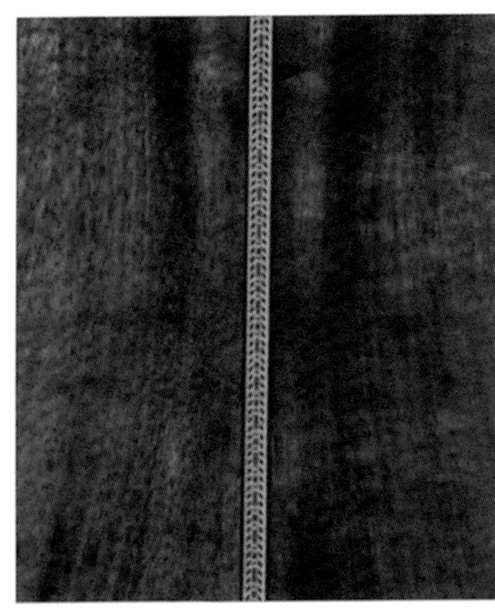

The OMC-16E's backstripe and binding contrast elegantly with its varnished koa back.

CFM (Martin) EM-18

The late 1970s were difficult times for acoustic guitar makers, as the cost of raw materials and labor rose, while the use of synthesizers and other electronics continued to grow. Martin responded to these problems by trying to break into the solid electric guitar market. The company introduced the CFMs in 1979. Initially, the range comprised two 6-stringers and a bass. An additional guitar and bass appeared in 1981.

They had contoured maple and walnut bodies. None of the CFM models sold particularly well, but the EM-18, which featured twin humbucking pickups with coil-taps and phase reverse switches, sold 1,375 examples between 1979 and 1983. All five CFM solid electrics were discontinued at this time.

The EM-18's pickups are powerful, high quality humbucking units.

Martin Alternative XT

Martin introduced the first-ever instrument in its "ALternative' range, the 00-size "X" model, in 2001. The capitalization of the L in its name is deliberate: AL is the scientific symbol for aluminum, which is used for the tops of the instruments in this series. Thanks to its exceptional strength, it requires much less internal bracing than a conventional wooden top.

The X model has a clear, responsive tone, both when played acoustically, and when the guitars' built-in electronics are plugged in. The ALternative XT featured here debuted in 2002. Constructed similarly to other models in the series, its most striking features are a Bigsby vibrato, a DiMarzio Fast Track 2 pickup, and a "graffiti pattern" on the aluminum.

The removable aluminum grille over the sound hole bears the famous Martin "CFM" initials.

Martin CF-1 Archtop

Dale Unger (b. 1954) grew up in the area around the C.F. Martin headquarters in Nazareth, Pennsylvania. He decided to specialize in archtop guitars and studied with Robert Benedetto. The famous guitar maker was then based in the little Pennsylvania town of East Stroudsburg. Dale Unger set up American Archtop Guitars in 1995, and started producing his own models, some of which were built using Benedetto's patterns and molds. The next stage of Unger's career began in 2001, when he approached Martin with a proposal for a new range of f-hole guitars that would blend Martin's craftsmanship with his archtop designs. Two Unger/Martin instruments, the CF-1 and the thinline CF-2, were launched in 2004.

Dale Unger and Christian Frederick Martin IV (Martin's Chairman and CEO) signed the label inside the CF-1's f-hole.

Martin BC-15E Acoustic Bass

Martin's first-ever basses, the EB-18 and EB-28 electrics (launched in 1979 and 1980), were not particularly successful. The company has had much more success with its recent bass guitars. This BC-15E is a recent addition to the 15 series, having debuted in 2000. This series, first introduced in 1935 had traditionally featured unbound mahogany bodies with a natural finish.

Today, Martin also uses sapele on their "most affordable solid wood guitars." The BC-15E is a sister model to the Dreadnought 6-string DC-15E. It has a 16-inch wide body that supplies a rich, mellow timbre, and one satisfied customer, bassist Eddie Foronda, referred to the guitar's pleasant "forest fragrance" that it has when new.

This close-up shows the substantial, robust bridge saddle (made from Tusq), and the pins required for the instrument's thick strings.

Martin 000-28LD Lonnie Donegan

Scotsman Lonnie Donegan (1931-2002) introduced audiences throughout the world to Skiffle, an exciting new genre, infused with elements of blues, folk, and country that swept Great Britain in the mid-1950s.

Skiffle music inspired both John Lennon and Paul McCartney of The Beatles to take up the guitar. In a career that spanned five decades, Donegan sold millions of records, and enjoyed massive success as a live performer. Lonnie was a long-time devotee of Martin guitars, and in early 2002, the company announced plans to honor him by producing a limited edition series of acoustics based on his favorite Martin model, the 000-28 he had played since 1967. These were the 000-28LD and the 000-28LDB.

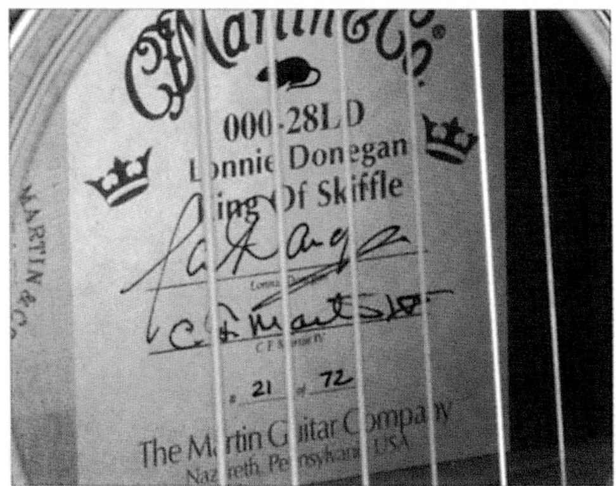

Each of the 72 limited edition 000-28LDs carries the signatures of Lonnie Donegan and Martin's Chairman and CEO, Chris Martin IV.

Martin 000-28EC Eric Clapton

A long-time devotee of Martin guitars, rock legend Eric Clapton first collaborated with the company on a limited edition model in 1995. This was the 000-42EC, whose design was partly based on Clapton's much-prized pre-Second World War 000-42. 461 of these were made; the number is a reference to Clapton's classic album 461 Ocean Boulevard. The following year saw the launch of a production "Signature Model" 000-28EC. The guitar has become a bestseller.

This is a recently made example. It has a spruce top with Indian rosewood back and sides, and boasts herringbone inlays. It also has an inlaid autograph of the great guitarist on its 20th fret. 000-42ECB was launched in 2000, and the 000-28ECB in 2002.

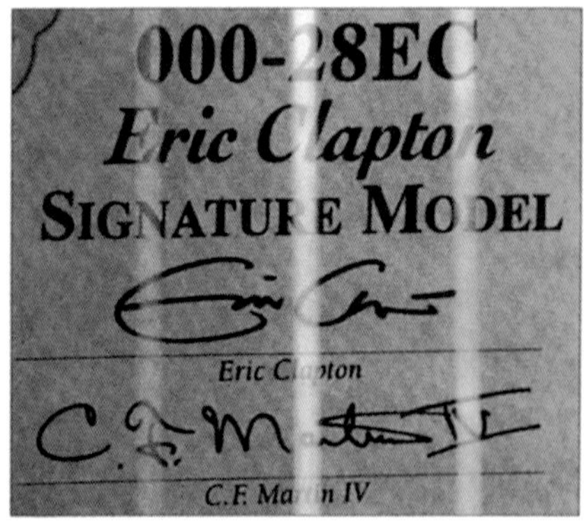

The label that appears in the limited edition of 461 guitars with Eric Clapton's signature. The number is a reference to Eric's classic 461 Ocean Boulevard album.

Martin HD-35SJC Judy Collins

Judy Collins made her name in the late 1960s as an unrivalled interpreter of classic songs such as Joni Mitchell's "Chelsea Morning" and "Both Sides Now." She has remained perennially popular as a singer, actress and author, and in 2002, Martin saluted her achievements, and her long-standing use of its instruments in the studio and onstage, with the release of two "signature edition" Judy Collins guitars. These were a 6-string model (as featured) and a 12-string. They are D-35 type models with Sitka spruce tops and Collins' "trademark" wildflower inlaid on their headstocks. Her Wildflower album of 1967 launched her songwriting career. Proceeds from the limited edition went to the United Nations Children's Fund.

Martin HD12-35SJC Judy Collins

Of the two Martin Judy Collins "signature edition" guitars, this 12-string model is perhaps the most personal to her. Its basic design is similar to the D12-35 Martin Dreadnought that she has performed with for many years. Like many folk-influenced singers of her generation, she was almost certainly inspired to take up the 12-string, whose rich, jangling sound is ideal for vocal accompaniment, after hearing it being used by Pete Seeger, and before him, Leadbelly. She has also frequently recorded with former Byrd Roger McGuinn, perhaps the most distinctive of the instrument's exponents. The Collins guitar combines fine woods with sonic excellence and outstanding decoration, including the columbine headstock inlay.

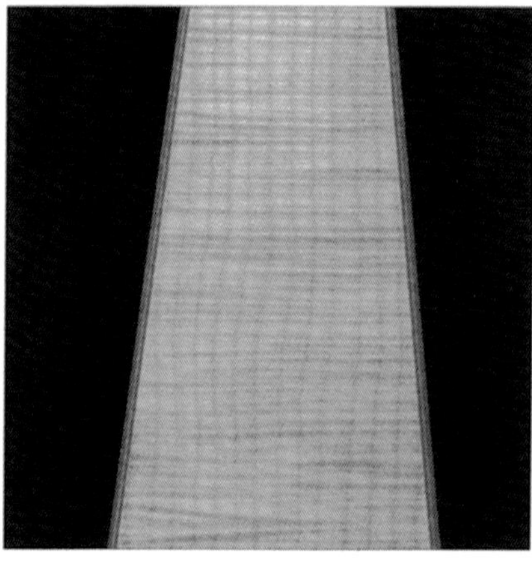

The heel perfectly matches the elegantly bordered central maple section of the instruments back.

Martin D-45
Mike Longworth

Mike Longworth was born in 1938, and grew up in Chattanooga, Tennessee. While still in high school, he developed a reputation for creating elaborate inlays on guitars and other fretted instruments. By the mid-1950s, his skills were being called upon by a succession of music stars. Among them was bluegrass great Lester Flatt. Word of Longworth's talents reached Martin, and the company took him on as an employee in 1968. One of his first jobs was to create the inlays for the relaunched D-45. His encyclopedic knowledge of Martin's guitars led to him publishing a definitive history of the company in 1975. After his death in 2003, Martin decided to honor Mike with a "Commemorative Edition" of only 91 guitars.

Mike Longworth's reputation for high quality inlays was unparalleled and his skills were celebrated in the commemorative edition that followed his death in 2003.

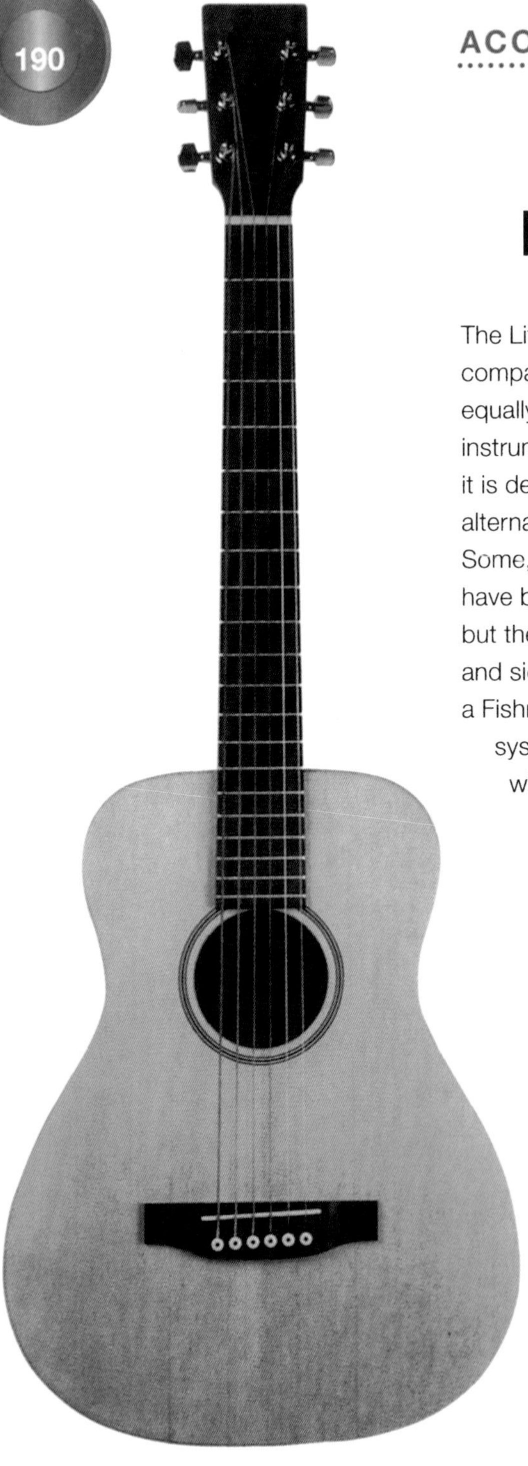

Martin Little Martin LX1E

The Little Martin was introduced in 2003. It is a robust, compact, ''go-anywhere'' flat-top acoustic, which is equally suitable for adults and children. Unlike some instruments of a similar size (it has a 23 inch scale length), it is designed to be played at a standard pitch. Several alternative types of the Little Martin guitar are available. Some, including the original LXM and LXME versions, have bodies made entirely from high pressure laminates, but the LX1E has a solid Sitka spruce top, with back and sides of ''mahogany pattern'' HPL. It is fitted with a Fishman-designed ''Mini Q'' under-saddle transducer system that delivers impressive ''plugged-in'' results when recording or playing through an amplifier.

This shot shows the layers of wood or HPL (high pressure laminate) that comprise the Little Martin's back, sides and neck.

Martin Cowboy III

Martin has a proud history, and a long-standing dedication to the highest standards of flat-top lutherie, but it also has a sense of humor. Among the more unusual instruments it launched in 2000 was the "Cowboy X," a limited edition model of 750 guitars decorated with a colorful "campfire scene" painting by artist Robert Armstrong. Armstrong's illustrations and cartoons (showcasing characters such as Mickey Rat and the Couch Potato) have graced magazines and books since the 1970s. Collaborating with Martin was especially enjoyable for Armstrong, as he is himself an accomplished guitarist and accordionist, who has appeared as a sideman with fellow cartoonist R. Crumb's Cheap Suit Serenaders.

The dog in Robert Armstrong's picture seems to be howling along to the tune being picked by the cowboy guitarist.

Martin 'Felix' Limited Edition

The cartoon character Felix The Cat made his debut in a movie short in 1919. Felix himself was created and originally drawn by Otto Messmer, but acquired a restyled look when Joe Oriolo took over the production of ''Felix'' artwork from Messmer. The lovable feline has proved perennially popular in a variety of different media, and in 2004, it was announced that Joe Oriolo's son Don had teamed up with the Martin company to produce a ' 'Felix'' guitar. The limited edition instrument (only 756 were produced), has a travel-size body made from high pressure laminates. Its back and sides are black, and its spruce-braced top is adorned with multiple Felix heads, as well as a ''Felix The Cat'' logo, and Don Oriolo's signature.

Don Oriolo, the son of Joe Oriolo, one of the original Felix illustrators, collaborated with Martin in 2004, to launch the ''Felix'' guitar.

Martin Backpacker

The Martin Backpacker's unique compact design allows it to be taken to places that would be strictly out of bounds to regular-sized acoustics. Since the first of these endearing little guitars (built for Martin in Mexico) rolled off the production line in 1991, they have been seen and heard in a string of exotic locations, from the South Pole to the Mount Everest Base Camp in Tibet.

Backpackers have even been taken onboard the US Space Shuttle Columbia, and are said to be a favorite among airline staff. Despite its small size, the Backpacker's 24-inch scale length and standard fingerboard width make it easy to play, though the narrow body does require a strap to keep it in position. It has clear, well-balanced tone.

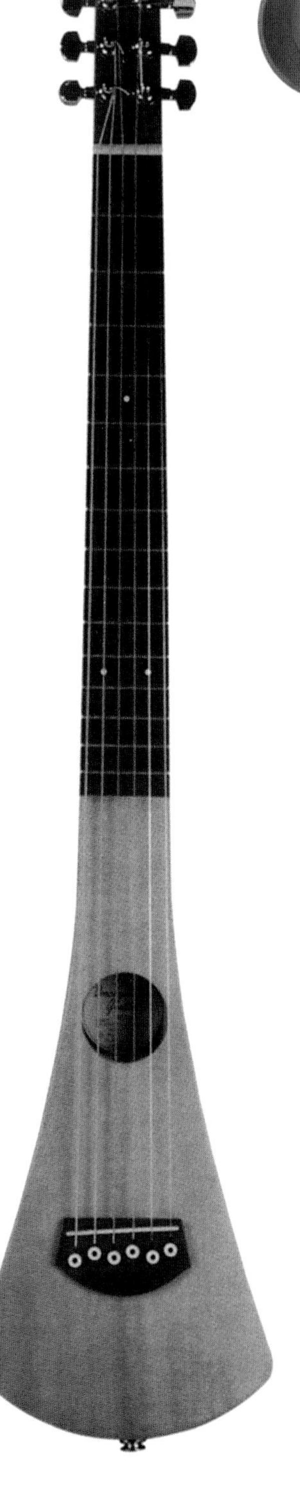

Brian May Signature

Unlike many leading rock guitarists, Brian May, who made his name with Queen in the 1970s and 80s, and was recently voted one of the world's top five players, has stayed largely faithfully to a single instrument throughout his long and distinguished career.

Even more unusually, he designed and built his favorite "Red Special" electric himself, with a little help from his father. The guitar dates from 1964: it was made with wood from a Victorian fireplace. The first official replica of the Ed Special was produced as a limited edition by Guild in 1984. The same company introduced a second Brian May model nine years later, but it was not until 2001 that an affordable version was launched by Burns London.

Each of the three pickups has a dedicated on-off switch, and, below it, a phase switch, allowing the creation of a wide variety of sounds.

Mosrite Ventures

Semie Moseley started building guitars in his teenage years, including a triple-neck model. He and his brother Andy founded Mosrite of California in 1956. At first, they produced custom guitars, but sales increased dramatically after Nokie Edwards of the Ventures endorsed their instruments. Barbara Mandrell also played Mosrites. But bad business decisions meant that the company went bankrupt in 1968, but they were back in business by 1970. This solid body electric has a Sunburst finish on its carved body. Its neck pocket is dated June 30, 1966. It also boasts a bound rosewood 22-fret fretboard, dot markers, and two pickups with "Mosrite of California" covers. The tailpiece and bridge are Moseleys, and the tuners are Klusons.

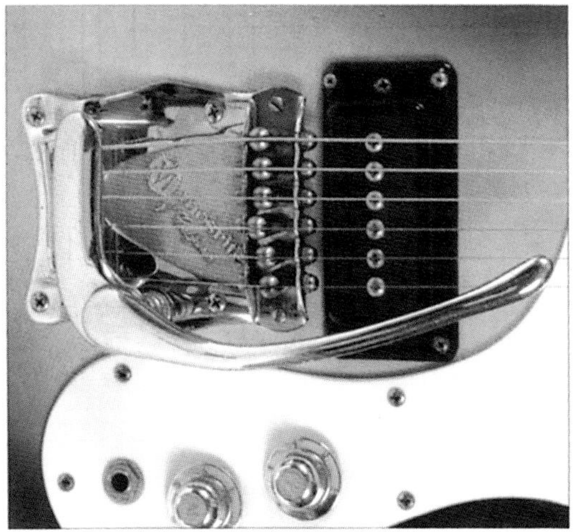

The guitar has two pickups with "Mosrite of California" covers, a Moseley tailpiece with vibrato, and a yellowed pickguard.

Music Man StingRay 5 Bass

Leo Fender co-founded Tri-Sonics in 1972, together with two former Fender staffers. The new company was renamed Music Man in February 1973. Music Man started out as a manufacturer of amplifiers, but introduced its first instrument, the StingRay bass, in 1976. The guitar had a particularly distinguished headstock design. Further basses and guitars followed. Like the StingRay, these were built at Leo Fender's own CLF factory (the initials stand for Clarence Leo Fender) in Fullerton, California. Sadly, Music Man's management soon became riven with tensions and personality clashes. By the end of the decade, Leo Fender had effectively ended his involvement with the business, and was planning a new venture, G&L.

A rear view of the StingRay 5's body: the instrument's neck plate carries its serial number and maker's trademarks.

Music Man Sub 1

The SUB 1 was launched in January 2004; a mid-price, though very impressively specified guitar, it was the third instrument in the SUB series. The range's name is derived from the initials of Sterling Ball, the company's president. Sterling's father, Ernie Ball, had acquired the company in 1984.

It is a matter of intense pride within Music Man that the SUBs are built at the firm's headquarters in San Luis Obispo, California, rather than overseas. Music Man's strategy is to use clever engineering and alternative materials to overcome the cost of domestic production. The SUB 1 is available in seven alternative textured colors, and with single or dual humbucking pickups. It weighs only 6 pounds 5 ounces.

Music Man Albert Lee

British guitarist Albert Lee (b. 1943) began his professional career as a teenager, quickly building a reputation for his country-influenced picking style. He was soon spending much of his time in the USA, where he performed with many famous groups and artists, including the late Buddy Holly's former group The Crickets, Emmylou Harris's Hot Band, Eric Clapton, and the Everly Brothers. Guitar Player has voted him "Best Country Guitar Picker" five times. Albert Lee's "signature" Music Man guitar began life as a prototype in the late 1980s, and has been commercially available since 1994. It features a distinctive shaped body made from ash, and three single coil pickups. This example is a "hard-tail."

This instrument is a "hard-tail" version (vibrato and bridge-mounted transducer versions are also available) and it has single coil pickups supplied by Seymour Duncan.

National Duolian

In the 1920s, a Los Angeles-based banjo maker, John Dopyera (1893-1988) found an ingenious solution to the perennial problems of audibility suffered by onstage acoustic guitarists when he created a new, louder type of instrument for a local vaudeville performer, George Beauchamp. It featured three aluminum resonators that gave extra projection to the vibrations picked up from its bridge, and in 1928, Dopyera, Beauchamp and other investors set up the National company to produce guitars, mandolins, and ukuleles incorporating these so-called "tri-cones."

The first National guitars appeared in 1928. These were wooden. Steel single-cones like this "Spanish"-necked Doulian guitar date from the mid-1930s.

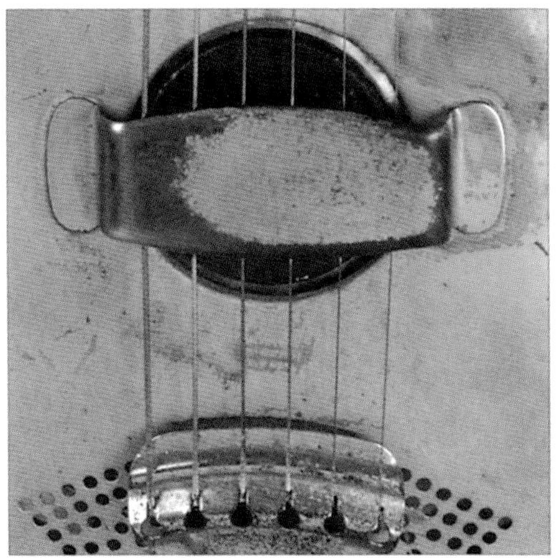

A maple "biscuit" under the string-guard transfers the vibrations to the single cone resonator, which amplifies the sound.

National Triolian

John Dopyera was the technical genius responsible for National's innovative resonator instruments: he held the patents for the tri-cone system that had brought the company its initial success, and was responsible for developing its single-cone counterpart.

A reserved, ascetic figure, he soon found himself at odds with the forceful, headstrong George Beauchamp, the firm's General Manager; and in 1929, their strained relations broke down when Beauchamp sought to claim the credit for inventing the single-cone resonator. This formed the background to the launch of this Triolian steel-body, single-resonator guitar. It was produced with painted finishes, the most simple of which is this "two-tone walnut" coloring.

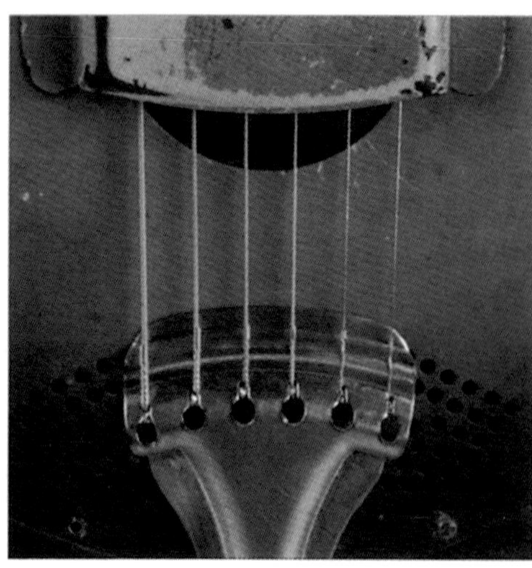

The steel used to make the Triolians was slightly heavier than that found on the Duolians.

National Rosita

Though National remained financially buoyant in the early 1930s, the company was in considerable turmoil. The principal cause of this was the legal action initiated by Dobro, who alleged that their rival resonator-making business had been damaged by false statements made by National's General Manager, George Beauchamp. Beauchamp was sacked from his post at National in 1931. The resolution of the dispute with Dobro led to a rapprochement between National and the Dopyera family. In July 1935 Dobro and National merged.

Under this new regime, National continued to make both metal-and wood-body resonator instruments, including the elegant birch plywood Rosita model illustrated here.

The Rosita's resonator cover is decorated very differently to those on the earlier Nationals.

National Cosmopolitan

The National guitar company moved its manufacturing base to Chicago in the mid-1930s. Now renamed Valco, the Chicago operation was soon making instruments for third parties such as catalog houses, as well as acoustics and electrics carrying the National brand name. The National solid-body shown here is a Cosmopolitan with a blond finish. The model first appeared in 1954, two years after a simpler, one-pickup electric National, called the Solid Body Electric Spanish, had made its debut. The range was almost certainly inspired by the success of Leo Fender's Telecasters. Like them, the guitar had a bolt-on neck, single cutaway, and a workmanlike appearance. They were widely used by blues players.

A threaded screw attaches the guitar's neck to the body and the pickup is attached to the pickguard with the wiring running beneath it.

National Reso-Phonic Delphi

National Reso-Phonic, based in San Luis Obispo, California, is recognized as the principal "torch-bearer" of the resonator instrument-making traditions. During their first few years in business for themselves, they were unable to afford the tooling needed to build metal guitar bodies, but eventually succeeded in putting their steel-bodied Delphi and brass Style O models into production in 1992. Their output now includes an impressive range of resonator guitars, mandolins, and ukuleles made in steel, brass, and wood.

The Delphi single-cone has been a perennial bestseller for National Reso-Phonic, and is currently available as a "standard" version, and a "Delphi Vintage Steel" model as featured here.

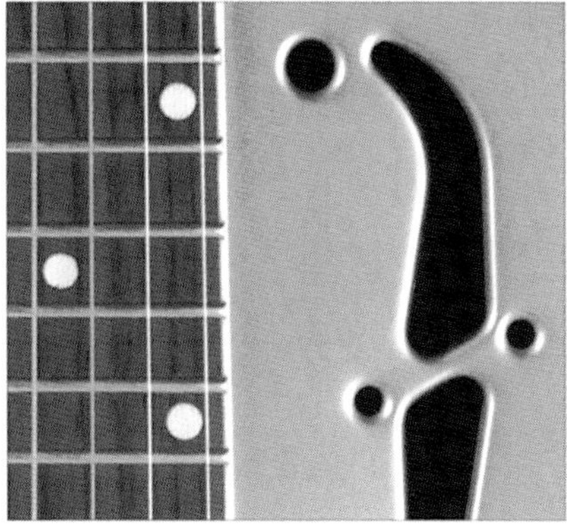

Ivoroid binding around the Delphi's hard rock maple neck and rosewood fingerboard, makes a striking contrast with its steel, satin nickel-finished, resonator cover.

National Radio-Tone

Though National Reso-Phonic is celebrated for its metal resonator guitars, the first instruments it produced in the years after its launch in 1988 were single-cone models with wooden bodies. The sonic difference between the two materials is a subtle one, but wood tends to mellow the sound a little, which some players prefer.

The Radio-Tone, with its maple sides and 12-fret-to-the body maple neck, draws some inspiration from an "old-time" National model, the 1928 Triolian; but other features, such as the strikingly attractive headstock with its echoes of the glamorous "Radio Days" of the 1920s and 30s, are all its own. Sadly, this model, the least expensive guitar in the company's range, is no longer in production.

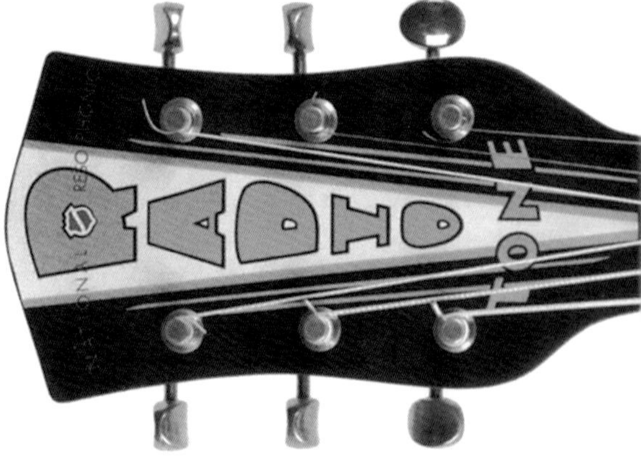

Don Young and McGregor Gaines created the Art Deco-influenced headstock design.

Ovation Viper

Ovation entered the conventional electric guitar market in 1968 with its "Electric Storm" range. This comprised seven semi-hollow models, including a 12-string and two basses, al of which were given appropriately "meteorological" names (Thunderhead, Tornado, Hurricane, Typhoon). The company's second generation of electrics was solid-bodies.

The Breadwinner (1972) and Deacon (1973) shared an asymmetrical shape, but the Preacher and Viper, dating from 1975, were more conventional-looking. The former sported a double cutaway and stereo circuitry, while the latter, shown here, had a simpler, single-cutaway design. It also had single-coil pickups, replaced by twin-coil units on this modified guitar.

Ovation B768 Elite Bass

The first ovation basses were electrics. Its 1968 catalog announced the introduction of two "Typhoon" slimline models with, respectively, one and two pickups, which were part of the company's "Electric Storm" range.

Today, Ovation basses all have acoustic bodies: the B768 model shown here is part of its "Elite" series, whose offset, miniature multi-soundholes, with their leafy "epaulets," resemble those found on Ovation Adamas guitars. However, unlike Adamas models, Elites have 100% wood tops made from either cedar or, in the case of the B768, spruce. A deep bowl is fitted to this bass, and its "plugged-in" sound is supplied via an OP24+ pre-amplifier with 3-band equalization. The model has now been discontinued.

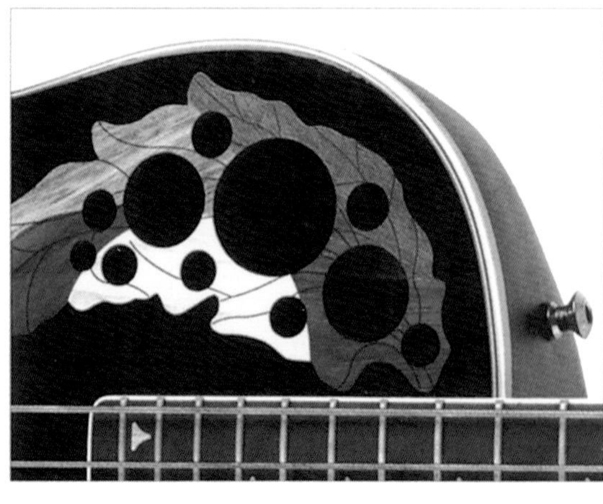

Elite series has a series of miniature multi-soundholes cut into its spruce top and decorated with leafy emblems.

Ovation CSD225-BCB Doubleneck

Double-necked guitars have a long history: as early as 1902, the Martin company had produced a two-neck harp guitar, and by the 1930s, Gibson was making electric Hawaiian models with twin necks that could each be tuned differently. Leo Fender took this concept even further, with his mid-1950s three- and four-necked Stringmaster Hawaiians. Ovation has recently introduced this production-model Celebrity Deluxe Doubleneck. Aware of the problems with size and weight that often dog the design of these guitars, the company has devised a scaled-down roundback body for it. It has a central cutaway, and has been fitted with a modified version of Ovation's OP24+ preamp system. The top is laminated spruce.

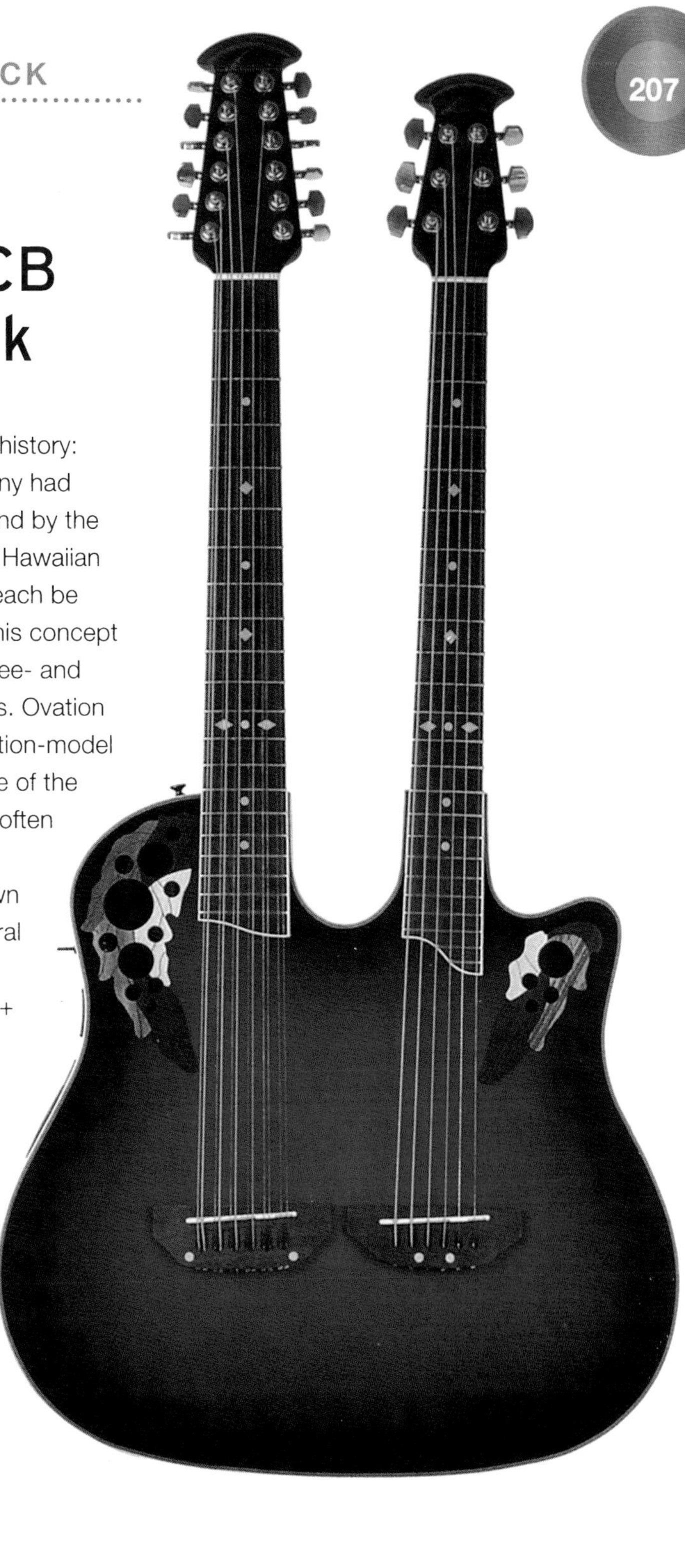

The two necks have rosewood fingerboards, and a 251/4-inch scale length. The guitar's bridge is walnut.

Ovation Tangent M.O.B.

Premium-price Ovations are built at Kaman's Connecticut headquarters, but Tangent models like this "M.O.B." model originate from Korea. The initials stand for "My Other Board." Ovation describes the guitar are a "rugged axe [that] can stand up to the stage, the beach, ad the street better than any other pro-quality acoustic." The guitar's "Blue Surf Burst" finish and board-shaped soundholes contribute to its informal, fun-looking image, but it is unquestionably a serious instrument, with no shortage of bright, powerful tone, especially when plugged into an amp or PA that can do justice to its impressively specified interna pickup system and OP30 preamp. Like most Ovations, it boasts a slimline neck, and spruce top.

Parker Fly Deluxe

Ken Parker made his first guitar, from wood and cardboard, aged 13. He went on to study various aspects of woodworking and tool making, and, while working in the New York area in the 1970s, gained valuable insights into instrument design from established experts such as lute builder Robert Meadow and archtop luthier Jimmy D'Aquisto.

These eclectic influences all contributed to the birth, in 1992, of the Parker Fly. The guitar is so named because it has an "exoskeleton" (like an insect's) of carbon and glass fiber over its wooden neck and body. As Parker has put it, "this structure allows us to sculpt a beautiful lightweight guitar, optimized for its ability to respond to the strings' vibrations."

The Fly's stainless steel frets are set directly into its keyboard. Despite being packed with sophisticated electronics the Fly weighs only about five pounds.

Parker P-44

Since the launch of the Fly, Parker's range has expanded to include new models such as Niteflys (featuring bolt-on necks instead of the complex "multifingered neck joints" used on the original Flys), as well as basses and even acoustics. In 2002, the company introduced its less expensive P-Series. This was a welcome development for players unable to afford thousands of dollars for one of Parker's premium guitars. Among the most successful of the "Ps" (whose construction is contracted out by Parker) is the P-44.

This model has recently been reintroduced after a period of absence from Parker's catalog. Like the Niteflys, the P-44 has a bolted neck (made from maple), a rosewood fingerboard, and dual pickup systems.

One of the humbucking pickups that create the P-44's distinctive sound. Immediately above it can be seen the end of the instrument's truss-rod.

Peavey Cropper Classic

Hartley Peavey set up Peavey Electronics in his hometown, Meridian, Mississippi, soon after graduating from college in 1965. It is now one of the world's largest manufacturers of musical instruments and sound equipment. Among Peavey's extensive guitar range is the highly acclaimed Cropper Classic. This was inspired and endorsed by notable Southerner, former Booker T. and the M.G.'s stalwart, Steve Cropper. Much of Cropper's searing guitar work was performed on a Fender Telecaster, and the Cropper Classic, introduced in the late 1990s, is similar in its outline and overall construction. Its electronics, though, are radically different, as it has two Peavey humbucking Blade units.

The guitar's gold-plated bridge is the "Db 4" bridge humbucker, three of whose four polepieces can be seen in the close-up.

Peavey Grind 5-String Bass

Over the last four decades, Peavey has won countless awards and accolades for its instruments and sound reinforcement gear, and its basses, which include student, mid-price, and professional models, are perennial bestsellers. This 5-string Grind was introduced in 2001. Like the 4-string Grind that debuted at the same time, it has an alder body and two passive, humbucking pickups. The transducers fitted to the 5-string are Peavey "J-styles" while the 4-stringer boasts both a J-style and a staggered-coil "P-style" unit inspired by those found on Fender's Precision Basses. Though the pickups are passive, the Grind also has an active, three-band EQ system, as well as treble boost, master volume, and blend controls.

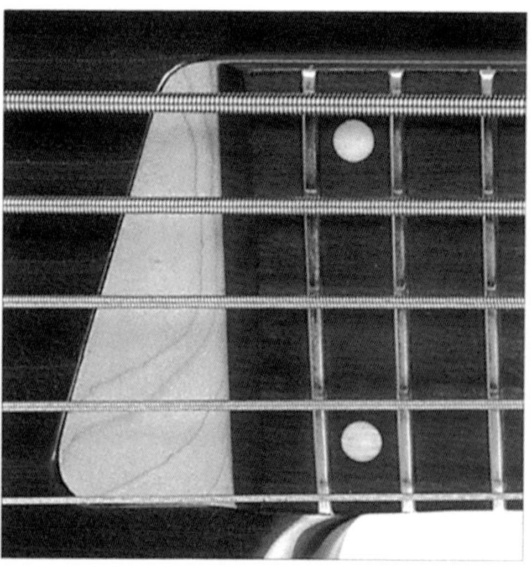

Pau Ferro ("iron wood") is used for the Grind's fingerboard.

Peavey JD-AG1

In 2004, Peavey announced that it had obtained an exclusive license to produce musical instruments and related equipment bearing the trademark of one of America's most celebrated whiskey makers, Jack Daniel's of Lynchburg, Tennessee. It is not known if Mr. Jack himself (1850-1911) was especially partial to music. However, he would surely have been pleased to see his brand promoted so ingeniously. Peavey-manufactured, Daniel's-adorned guitars and amps began to appear in Summer 2005. This guitar is one of the three acoustics that are currently available, the JD-AG1. It has a spruce top, mahogany back, neck, and sides, and a built-in Piezo pickup. It is intended to appeal to Jack Daniel's enthusiasts and music fans alike.

Peavey Jack Daniel's Electric EXP

To complement their three Jack Daniel's acoustic guitars, Peavey has introduced no less than five electric models. The most expensive of these are equipped with striking extras such as truss rod and switch covers made from pieces of the famous distiller's wooden whiskey barrels! These are not present on this Jack Daniel's Electric EXP, but this slightly cheaper instrument has many other desirable features. It is fitted with Peavey's patented Dual-Compression tailpiece, two powerful humbucking pickups, and a quilted maple top to its mahogany body. It also has chromed hardware, an ebony fingerboard, and a JD logo on the headstock. Two finishes are available, "Transparent Whiskey" and "Transparent Charcoal."

Even the guitar's control knobs have the "Old No. 7" brand engraved on them!

PRS Custom 24

The Custom 24 has a very special place in the history of Paul Reed Smith Guitars. Developed through lengthy trial and experimentation, during which Reed Smith, who had built his first guitar as a student, would craft instruments at his workshop in Annapolis, Maryland, "road-test" them at gigs, and then seek to sell them to musicians at local concert venues, it was this model that helped him obtain enough advance orders to launch the company bearing his initials in 1985.

The company now describe the model as "the core of our line." They have carved maple tops and mahogany backs. PRS is now acclaimed as one of America's most distinguished guitar makers. Carlos Santana was an early Reed Smith client.

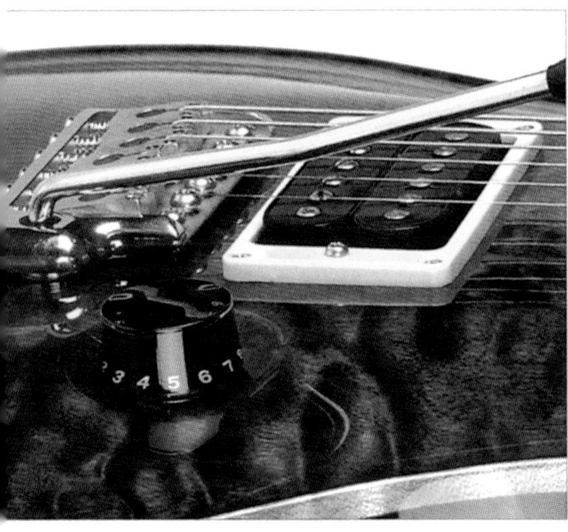

The bridge pickup is a PRS HFS model; the initials stand for "hot, fat, and screams."

PRS Corvette

This 2005 PRS guitar is an homage to America's greatest sports car, the Chevrolet Corvette. It is based on the PRS Standard 22, but features a Corvette banner and iconic red finish. Its shorter neck contributes to a particularly warm tone. The guitar has a "Victory Red" finish with a racing flag graphic.

It has a 25-inch scale length, and a carved mahogany body with a wide-fat neck profile, together with a 22-fret rosewood fingerboard with a custom Z06 inlay. The instrument has two Dragon II humbucking pickups (treble and base) with nickel silver covers, nickel hardware, and a wraparound bridge and tailpiece. It is also equipped with Phase II locking tuners. The instrument is supplied with a hardshell case.

Set on the top (finished in Victory Red) is the Chevrolet Corvette Z06 racing flags logo.

PRS Electric Bass

Paul Reed Smith's initial foray into electric bass production took place in 1986 with the Bass-4 and Bass-5. These 4- and 5-stringers shared the elegant looks and luxurious woods and inlays of the company's standard guitars, but were not very warmly received by critics or players, and were dropped in 1991.

In 2000, a second generation model, named simply the PRS Electric Bass, was introduced: plainer and more functional than its predecessors, it had an alder body, a bolted on maple neck, and two passive pickups whose exposed blades were shaped to follow the radius of the instrument's fingerboard. The firm's publicity described their tone as ''fat and clear,'' A piezo transducer was fitted a month later.

The abalone dots on the fingerboard are less elaborate than many decorations found on other PRS guitars.

PRS McCarty Hollowbody II

IN 1998, Paul Reed Smith introduced a series of guitars inspired by the classic, E-335-style thinline/semi-solids that had been developed by Gibson in the late 1950s during Ted McCarty's time. The new instruments were named ''McCarty Hollowbodies,'' but there were considerable differences between the Gibsons and the PRS electrics. Semi-solids such as the ES-335 contain central wooden block that reduces feedback and increases sustain. PRS replaced it with a single ''sound post'' running beneath the bridge/tailpiece units. There are three currently available PRS McCarty Hollowbodies: the Hollowbody Spruce, Hollowbody I, and Hollowbody II. The latter has a maple top and back.

A single ''sound post'' runs beneath the guitar's bridge and tailpiece units coupling together the top and back sections of the instrument. Its pickups are PRS ''McCarty Archtop'' units.

PRS Single Cutaway

Paul Reed Smith started making guitars in high school, and started making guitars for a living out of college. He started by making them one at a time, and counted himself lucky if he could produce one each month. Befriending roadies gave him the opportunity to sell his guitars, backstage, to several stars, including Carlos Santana, Al Di Meola, and Howard Leese. With a strong team of craftsmen and financial backers, Paul Reed Smith started the company that bears his name, and continues to run it today. This single cutaway artist package instrument was made to celebrate PRS's twentieth anniversary. It has a mahogany neck and body, carved one-piece quilted maple top, rosewood fretboard, and shell inlays.

The gold hardware looks great against the Blue Matteo satin finish on the flamed maple. Note the paua shell bird inlays on the fingerboard.

PRS SE Soapbar

PRS's "SE" range is designed at its headquarters in Stevensville, Maryland, but manufactured in Korea. SE instruments, some of them variants of the company's premium models, are exceptionally good value, and the Soapbar SE seen here is of particular interest because of the lengthy battles triggered by its "Singlecut" body shape.

The firm first used the Singlecut design, which boasts one cutaway instead of the two found on many other PRS instruments, in 2000. Its introduction led to a lawsuit from Gibson, centering on its alleged similarity to the latter company's classic Les Paul guitar body. Aside from their body shapes, the old and new Soapbar SEs are very similar. Both feature twin "soapbar" pickups.

PRS Swamp Ash Special

Swamp Ash is mostly grown in the southern states of the USA, and is appreciated by guitar makers for its relatively lightweight, as well as its musical qualities. It is used to splendid effect on the Paul Reed Smith Swamp Ash Special, which has been in continuous production since 1996.

The model's pickups are also worthy of comment. Its neck and bridge humbuckers are "McCartys," named for former Gibson president Ted McCarty, the man behind the creation of the Les Paul and other famous designs. McCarty, who died in 2001, shared some of his lifetime's knowledge of lutherie and electronics with PRS in its early years. This instrument is finished in "Opaque Black." It was made in 2000.

Radiotone Archtop, c.1935

The introduction of the Gibson L-5 archtop acoustic in 1922 opened up a new role for the guitar as a rhythm and solo instrument in jazz and swing ensembles. European manufacturers, like Gibson's American competitors, were soon turning out archtops that replicated its features. This Radiotone instrument is likely to have been made in Germany. Definite information about brand is hard to find, but Radiotone ukuleles are known to have been in circulation in Britain before World War II. This instrument is an elegantly finished, high quality instrument. It would have suited a busy professional who lacked the funds for a Gibson or an Epiphone. One British "name" performer, Jack McKechnie, used a Radiotone in the 1930s.

This guitar is extremely well made, as shown by this detail of the fancy tuners, and would have suited a player who lacked the funds for a Gibson.

Regal Square-Neck Resonator

An Indianapolis music storeowner, Emil Wulschner, first used the Regal trade name in the late 1890s. In the wake of a sales slump, Chicago-based Lyon & Healy next acquired the marque. They began to produce Regal guitars in 1908. Over the next six decades, the marque changed hands several times. The company's most significant guitars were the Dobro resonators that it built between 1934 and about 1940. Regal suspended guitar production during World War II. Although production resumed after the war, its Chicago factory closed in 1968. The trademark remained dormant until 1987 when Saga Musical Instruments took it over. They offer an impressive selection of guitars, including this square-neck Dobro-type.

The Regal brand originated in the late 1890s, and has appeared on a wide variety of instruments since then.

B. C. Rich Mockingbird

B.C. Rich was a Los Angeles-based luthier who started out building high-end acoustics, but diversified into solid electrics in the late 1960s. Within a few years, his guitars were sporting increasingly sophisticated onboard electronics and neck-through-body designs; they were also beginning to assume the bold outlines.

The first of these shapes, the "Seagull," debuted in 1972; the "Mockingbird" profile of this recently manufactured instrument was introduced in 1976. The Rich Bich debuted in the same year. The featured Mockingbird is one of the company's "Body Art" series of "graphically enhanced" guitars. This range was launched in 2003. Bruce Krober's "Forty Lashes" design is from 2004.

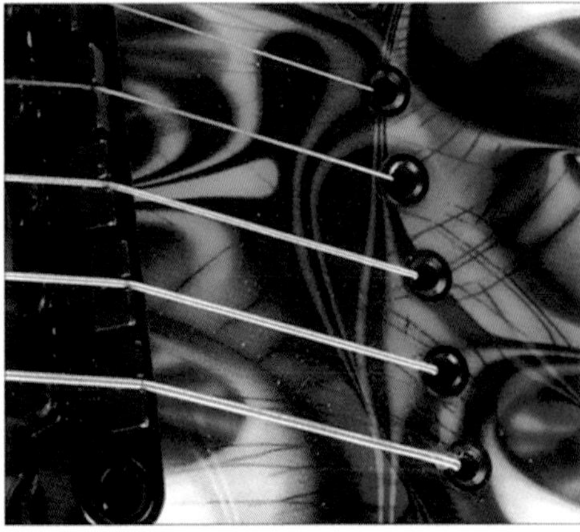

The guitar's basic shape has not changed since the 1970s, though its hardware and psychedelic finish are new.

B. C. Rich Virgo

Demand grew for B.C. Rich guitars throughout the late 70s and 80s, and the emergence of the heavy metal movement, with its appetite for high quality, visually arresting instruments, was a particular boon to the company. Before long, however, high demand meant that the company started to outsource some of their manufacturing. In 1983, the first full line of Japanese-made Riches, named the "N.J. Series" made its debut.

The initials stand for "Nagoya, Japan." N.J. production was moved to Korea later in the decade. Among the axes available in overseas-made versions during the mid-1980s was the Rich "Virgin:" it remains in the catalog to this day. This model is a more recent take on this classic design.

The Virgo's distinctive shape is said to look like a mid-1980s "Rich Virgin" with a bite out of its bottom!

B. C. Rich Dagger

In 1987, the New Jersey-based Class Axe company began distributing B.C. Rich's Korean-made guitar lines. Two years later, Class Axe licensed the Rich trademark. A Rich catalog from 1996 demonstrates the remarkable variety of instruments offered by the company during this period. These included the US-built Signature Series electrics (which included new versions of the Bich and Mockingbird), a well as more affordable Elite and N.J. models constructed in the Far East.

Today, B.C. Rich remains a top brand for hard rock and heavy metal players. This model is the competitively priced Special Edition Dagger. A semi-solid, it was introduced in 2005. It takes it names from its knife-shaped soundholes.

The Dagger has two "BDSM" humbucking pickups and mother-of-pearl fingerboard markers like pointed knife blades, which fit with the guitar's design theme.

Rickenbacker Electro Model B Lap Steel

The origins of the Rickenbacker company lie in the Ro-Pat-In Corporation, formed in Los Angeles in 1931 by Swiss-born Adolph Rickenbacker (1882-1976). The company developed an aluminum-bodied lap steel, nicknamed the ''Frying Pan,'' which appeared in 1932. This was the world's first mass-made electric guitar.

Ro-Pat-In was renamed Electro in 1934, and went on to make some ''Spanish''-style electrics, but focused most of its energy and resources on Hawaiian instruments such as the ''Model B'' seen here. Its body and neck are made from Bakelite (and were bolted together), which was less affected by temperature changes that could affect tuning than the aluminum used on the Frying Pan.

A detail view of the massive magnet on the pickup, which was designed by Electro's George Beauchamp.

Rickenbacker 330

Founder Adolph Rickenbacker remained at the company until 1953, when he sold the concern to F.C. Hall, a man with an impressive music industry track record, who had previously been involved in the distribution of Fender guitars. Under his leadership, Rickenbacker (as the business was now known) was soon introducing models that would attract an enthusiastic new generation of customers to the company.

The most iconic of these designs were the "300" series of thinline hollowbodies launched in 1958. Roger Rossmeisl, who had qualified as a guitar maker in Germany and was a former Gibson staffer, had created these. This instrument is a Rickenbacker 330, and has a "Mapleglow" finish.

Rickenbacker 360

All thinline Rickenbacker 300s are made from maple, have rosewood fingerboards, and share the same bodies shapes and depth (this was standardized at 11/2 inchs in 1962). Their principal differences relate to quantities of frets (21 or 24), numbers of pickups (2 or 3), presence of absence of vibrato, and types of decoration, all of which are categorized by the numerical codes by which the guitars are known. 21-fret necks are restricted to models numbered 310 to 325. These, together with lower-ranking 300s (up to 345) are "standard" thinlines. They have no bindings and only plain dot fret markets. However, instruments coded 360 and above, like this one from 1976, are classified as "deluxe" and boast extra decorative touches

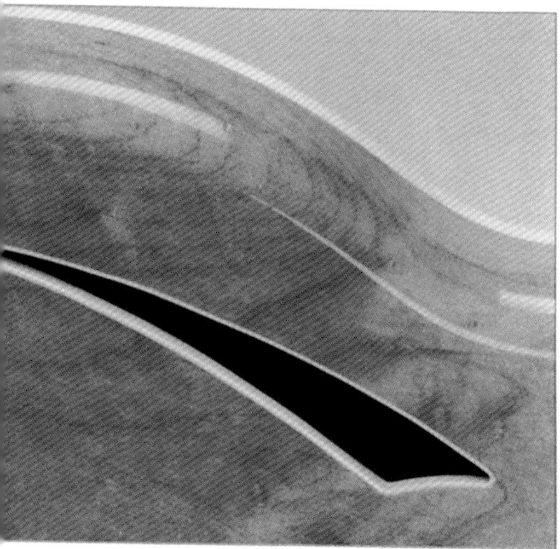

Rickenbacker's stylized f-holes (with cream bindings on this deluxe model) add to the guitar's visual appeal.

Rickenbacker 360/12VP 12-String

Rickenbacker announced its first electric 12-string guitars, including the 360/12, in 1963; they were introduced the following year, and early adopters included The Beatles' George Harrison, and Jim (later Roger) McGuinn of The Byrds. The 360/12 shares the normal features of its 6-string Series 300 counterparts, including a 24-fret neck and 11/2 inch body depth.

Perhaps its most striking innovation was the re-ordering of the string pairs that caused their lower-octave notes to be sounded first on a downstroke; other companies' 12-string groupings place the higher-pitched strings before the lower ones. The Schaller tuners are mounted from both the back and sides of the headstock, an ingenious space-saving feature.

Rickenbacker 4001 Bass

Rickenbacker's first electric bass, the 4000 was a single-pickup model with a comparatively unadorned appearance. It was introduced in 1957, and was joined just four years later by the twin-pickup 4001, which boasted neck and body bindings, as well as triangular fingerboard markers (the 4000 had only dot inlays).

From around 1963, the 4001 also featured the latest version of the company's distinctive string mute, whose dampers, located in the instrument's bridge/tailpiece assembly, could be raised and lowered by means of two thumbscrews (unfortunately the 4001 in the photograph has lost one of these). The 4001, like Rickenbacker's 6-string guitars, benefited considerably from its association with The Beatles.

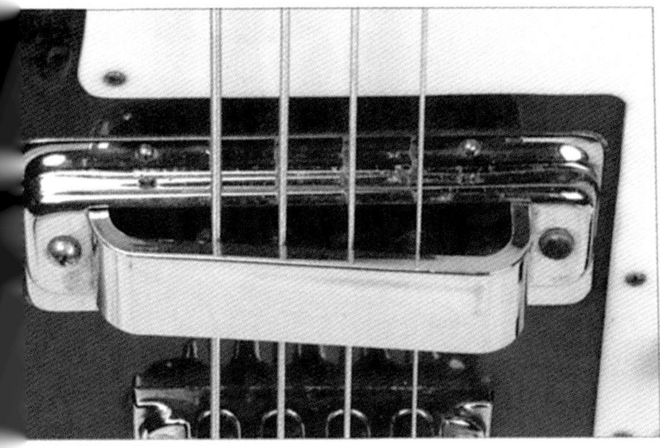

The intrusively positioned cover over the back pickup is not to every players taste and can be removed without unduly affecting the character of this 1960s classic.

Schecter Dream Machine

In 1976, David Schecter, a Southern California-based guitar customizer and repairer set up Schecter Guitar Research in order to produce high performance replacement pickups and other components. The following year, the company published a catalog showcasing an extensive range of substitute transducers, among which were ready-wired assemblies of coil-tapped pickups for Fender Telecasters and Stratocasters. Before long, Schecter was making guitar bodies and necks as well as electronics. It was only a matter of time before the company began using these as the basis for complete guitars, including the Dream Machine. This model dates from before 1982. It has a Strat-like outline, switching options, and six-point vibrato.

Silvertone 1448 Electric

Sears, Roebuck & Company of Chicago first used its "Silvertone" brand name on a wind-up phonograph in 1915; a few years later; the logo began to appear on Sears radios. In the 1930s, the company applied it to musical instruments, which had previously carried the "Supertone" marque. Silvertones were supplied to Sears by a number of different manufacturers, known in the trade as "jobbers." The first electric Silvertones came from Danelectro in New Jersey. This instrument dates from 1964, and incorporates typical Nathan Daniel touches like the "lipstick-tube" pickup, and metal and rosewood bridge. It was 1448 in the Sears catalog, and was supplied in a hardboard case with built-in amplifier and loudspeaker.

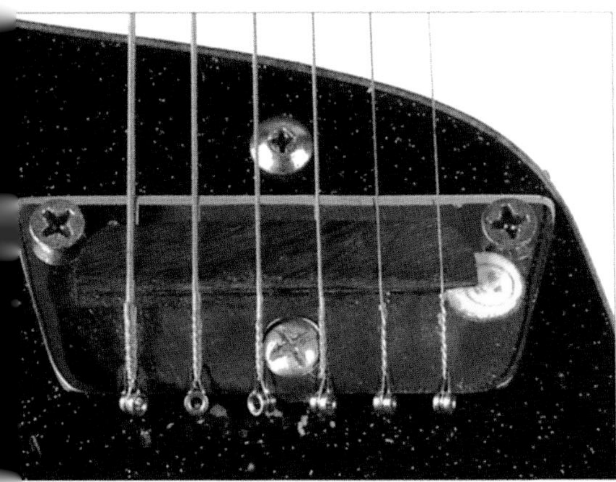

The metal and rosewood bridge, detailed in this close-up, is a typical Nathan Daniel design feature, as is the famous "lipstick-tube pickup."

Ken Smith BT Custom 6 Bass

Session musician Ken Smith formed the bass building firm that carries his name in 1978. Located in Perkasie, Pennsylvania. It has gone on to establish an enviable reputation for producing high-end instruments, and is especially noted for the quality of its woods.

Smith's range of basses includes this BT Custom 6, which is a neck-through-body design. Its center section is a five-layer "sandwich" of aged hardrock maple and bubinga, while its body "wings" are made with shedua, a very dense brown wood, grown in west and central Africa, which is reckoned to be some 130% harder than some species of oak. The BT also boasts a QSR (Quick String Release) bass bridge, 24-fret neck, and twin Smith "soapbar" pickups.

This Smith BT bass is several years old, but surprisingly, its bridge shows comparatively few signs of wear and tear.

Squier 'Obey' Telecaster

The "Squier" trademark was acquired by Fender from the V.C. Squier string-making firm in 1965 and, since 1983, has been used as a brand name for budget-priced, mostly Far Eastern-manufactured versions of the great American guitar company's instruments. Its "OBEY" range, launched in 2006, features graphic finishes by American artist Shepard Fairey, are striking and highly original. Fairey (b.1970) made his name as the creator of posters and street art bearing Orwellian slogans such as "Obey," and "You Are Under Surveillance." The artwork was applied to a special series of Squier Telecasters and Stratocasters. The dull finish of the tuners and other metalwork created an effective contrast to the body.

The matt finish of the adjustable bridge, control panel and tuners creates an effective contrast with the graphic-laden body.

Steinberger L2 Bass

New York-based furniture designer Ned Steinberger befriended luthier Stuart Spector in the late 1970s. He became fascinated with guitar design, and took a key role in developing Spector's NS-1 electric bass (1977). Steinberger then began to build his own basses.

Aware of the inherent tendency for heavy headstocks to create an uncomfortable imbalance, he adopted a radical solution. This was the complete removal of the peghead, and the repositioning of the tuners at the instrument's bridge end. He was also dissatisfied with the sound produced by wooden basses, and began to fabricate prototypes from graphite-reinforced epoxy resin. The experimentation resulted in the "headless" single-pickup L1 bass of 1979.

The Steinberger has no neck joint; its neck and body are formed from a single piece of resin. Its nut is also a string anchor.

Steinberger L2 Fretless Bass

Ned Steinberger's bold L1 (1979) and L2 (1981) bass designs quickly attracted interest from prominent players. These included John Entwistle of The Who, and King Crimson star Tony Levin. Widespread media attention generated huge demand for Steinbergers, including a newly introduced headless 6-string guitar and a fretless bass similar to this one.

In 1980, Ned Steinberger set up the Steinberger Sound Corporation to produce the L1. As the decade progressed, managing the company became an increasingly onerous task for its founder. Ned turned to Gibson's boss, Henry Juszkiewicz, for some business advice, and their discussions led to the 1987 purchase of Gibson by the Nashville-based guitar giant.

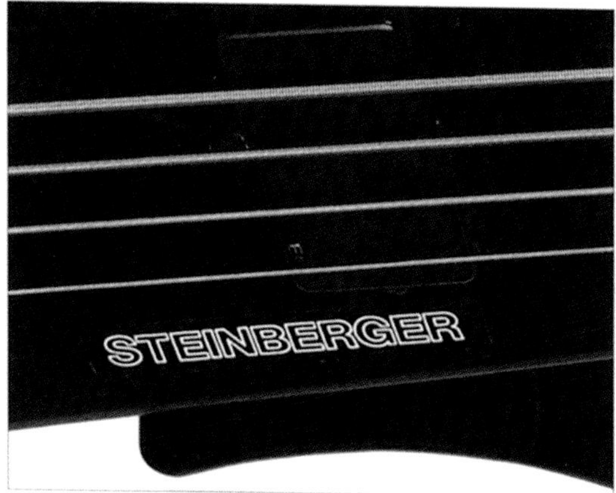

Declared one of the "Five Best Designs" of 1981 by Time magazine, the Steinberger even has a removable leg rest for seated players.

Tacoma Papoose

Tacoma guitars are now the third largest in the US (after Martin and Taylor). The company had its origins in a Japanese-owned wood-processing firm, the Sound Mill, set up in the early 1990s in Tacoma, Washington State, to produce soundboards for pianos.

The company also supplied woods to luthiers throughout America, and launched its own Tacoma brand guitars in 1997. The first of these was the Papoose, an unusual small-bodied instrument with a raised pitch, a perfect fourth higher than a standard guitar. It also has an offset "paisley"-shaped soundhole and contoured bridge. Tacoma builds its instruments using a combination of traditional craftsmanship and computer numeric control (CNC) technology.

The Tacoma's distinctive bridge plate is also found on the normal size guitars in the company's range.

Tacoma Chief

The Tacoma Chief is a single cutaway "mini-jumbo" with a solid Western cedar top, plus a back and sides of solid mahogany. It delivers a powerful sound that belies its relatively small size. Its bridge and 22-fret fingerboard are rosewood, its tuning machines chrome, and its bolted-on neck mahogany.

The standard version, seen here, has a natural finish and no on-board electronics. Other colors are available as optional extras, and the Chief can be supplied with three different pickup systems (by, respectively, L.R. Baggs, Fishman, and B-Band), at an additional cost of between $150 and $250. The Tacoma "Wing" series also includes larger-bodied regular and baritone guitars and basses, as well as two mandolins.

Thanks to the Chief's unconventional sound hole shape and location on the upper bass bout, its label has had to be re-sited.

Taylor T-5 Standard

The T-5, which made its debut in 2005, is Taylor's first-ever electric guitar. Aimed at players seeking to obtain both clear, acoustic-sounding tones and "hotter," overdriven timbres from a single instrument.

It contains three transducers, and an active pre-amp system that gives precise control over the sounds they provide. Standard T5s, like this one, have chrome fittings and dot inlays. "Artist" versions feature gold-plated hardware and more intricate fret-markers. Both models are offered with Sitka spruce, koa, or (as shown here) maple tops. Sapele wood is used for the backs and sides of all versions of the instrument. The necks of the T5s are constructed from tropical American mahogany.

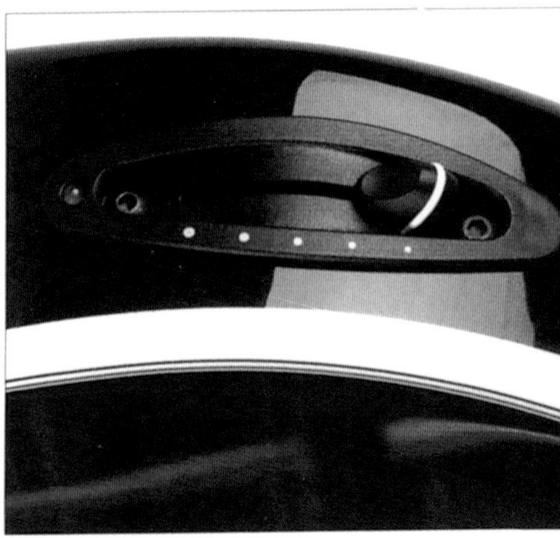

A close-up showing the T-5's 5-way pickup selector (with its associated LED) as well as the smart white binding which contrasts well with the maple in this "Cherry Sunburst" finish.

Tokai FV 40

The Tokai company was set up in Hamamatsu, Japan (also the hometown of Yamaha) in 1947, by businessman Tadayouki Adachi. Initially a harmonica manufacturer, it diversified into guitar production in the 1960s. By the mid-70s, Tokai was producing a range of flat-tops and electrics whose designs closely resembled those of Gibson and Martin. Tokai also made replicas of 1950s-style Les Pauls.

The company's guitars started to be sold in America in about 1983, and soon acquired a reputation for quality and value. After a period out of the limelight, Tokai is currently undergoing something of a renaissance, and this Flying V-like FV 40 comes from an extensive batch of electrics and acoustics that have debuted recently.

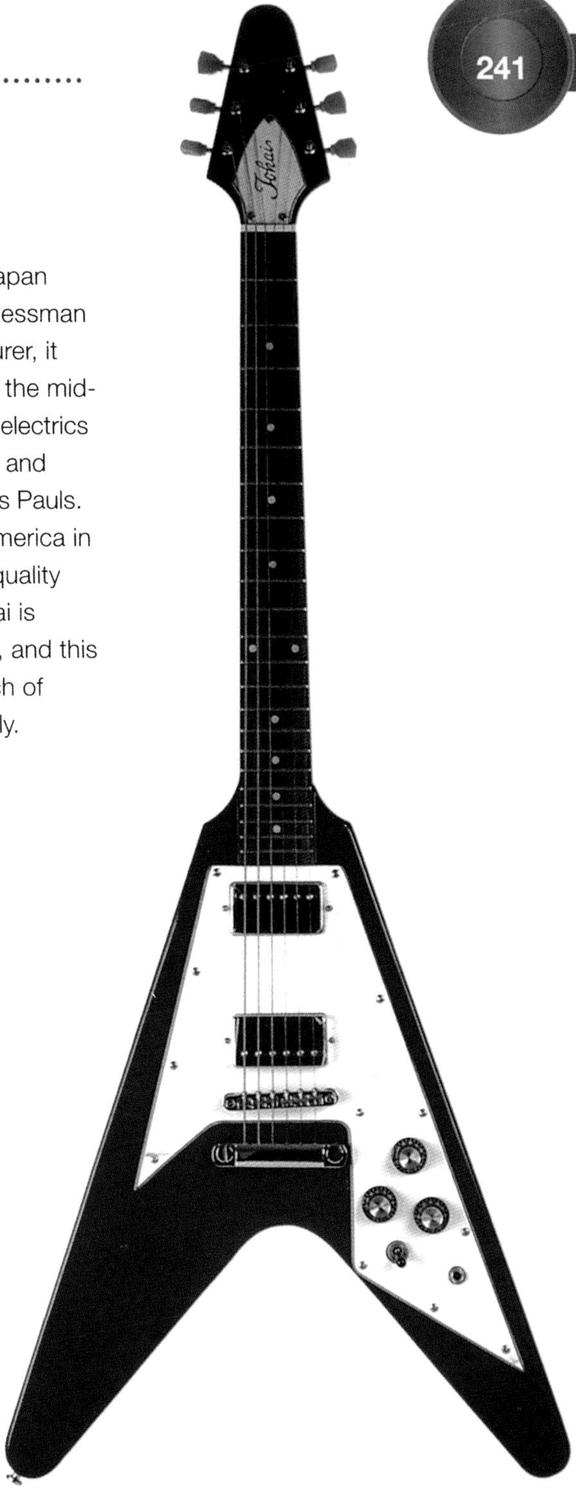

Valco Reso-Phonic

Beginning in 1941, and continuing until 1964, Valco put individual serial numbers on all its guitars. These appeared on a small aluminum plate nailed onto the back of the neck, near the peghead. This instrument is numbered X59792 which makes it a 1956 guitar. Included in this series were instruments that Valco manufactured for Sears (Silvertone), Montgomery Ward (Airline), and Oahu. Songwriter/guitarist Jeff Lang, who has quite an extensive collection of various instruments, describes this model as a "curious little guitar." Made by the National Guitar Company, this example has synthetic red body covering, a 22-inch scale, and a 20-fret rosewood fingerboard, complete with pearl dot inlays.

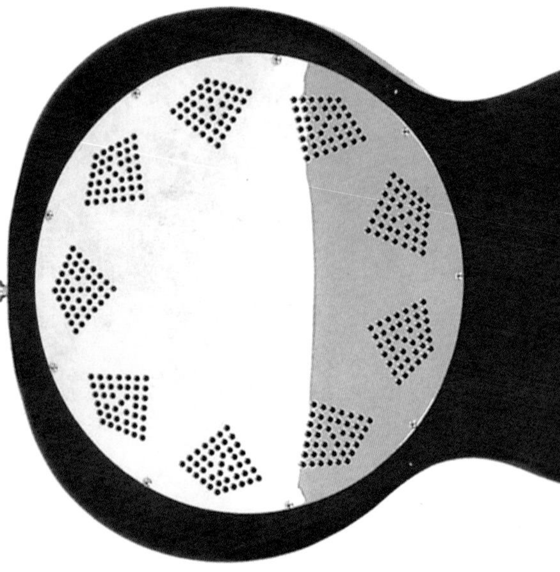

The 10-inch sieve resonator coverplate design is replicated on the back of the Valco.

Vigier Arpege

Patrice Vigier set up his guitar- and bass-making company in 1980, after several years of experience as an instrument repairer. From the start, the designs he produced in Grigny, France, were bold and challenging.

They included the Surfreter fretless electric, and the bass shown here. Versions of both remain in production. Among the key features that make Vigier basses special are their pickups (highly responsive units designed by the late Michel Benedetti), and the composition of their necks, which are constructed from 90% wood and 10% carbon. The carbon takes the place of a controversial truss-rod. High-profile players of exclusive Vigier instruments include Adam Clayton of U2 and Roger Glover of Deep Purple.

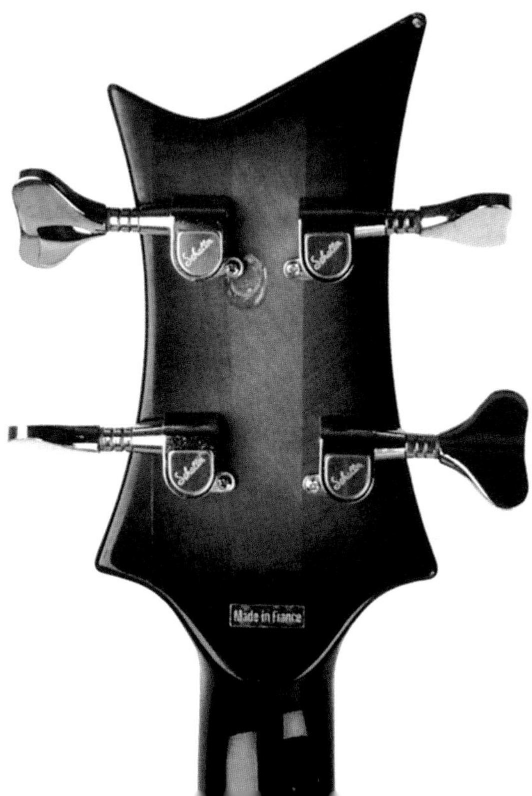

Watkins Circuit 4

Londoner Charlie Watkins developed a range of instrument amplifiers and P.A. systems in the years following World War II. These were marketed under the WEM (Watkins Electric Music) marque. By the end of the 1950s, Watkins had diversified into electric guitar manufacturing. These were largely the work of Charlie's brother Reg. While influenced by the work of Leo Fender, they sometimes featured a bewildering proliferation of electronic gadgetry.

But many of their products were competitively priced and highly successful, especially among ''entry-level'' players. This Watkins Circuit 4 dates from 1964. It is an attractive period piece, whose good condition and comparative rarity make it highly collectible.

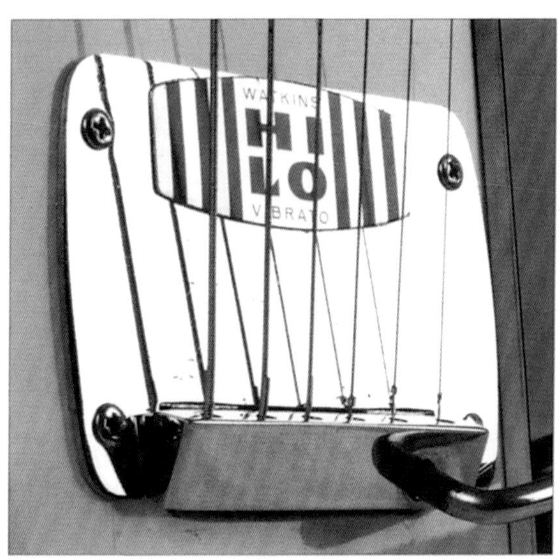

A close-up of the simple but effective ''HiLo'' vibrato, which is also featured on several of Watkins's other instruments.

Wechter Pathmaker

Abe Wechter first attracted widespread attention in the mid-70s, while he was working at Gibson, where he was involved in the creation of a special acoustic guitar for John McLaughlin. He established a lutherie business of his own in Paw Paw, Michigan, where he went on to build custom instruments for a number of top players, including John McLaughlin and top Swedish bassist Jonas Hellborg.

In 1994, Wechter completed the prototype of his distinctive "Pathmaker" double-cutaway flat-top, and, three years later, he set up a manufacturing facility to produce it in greater quantities. It is currently available in a variety of versions. "Elite" Pathmakers are custom crafted in Paw Paw.

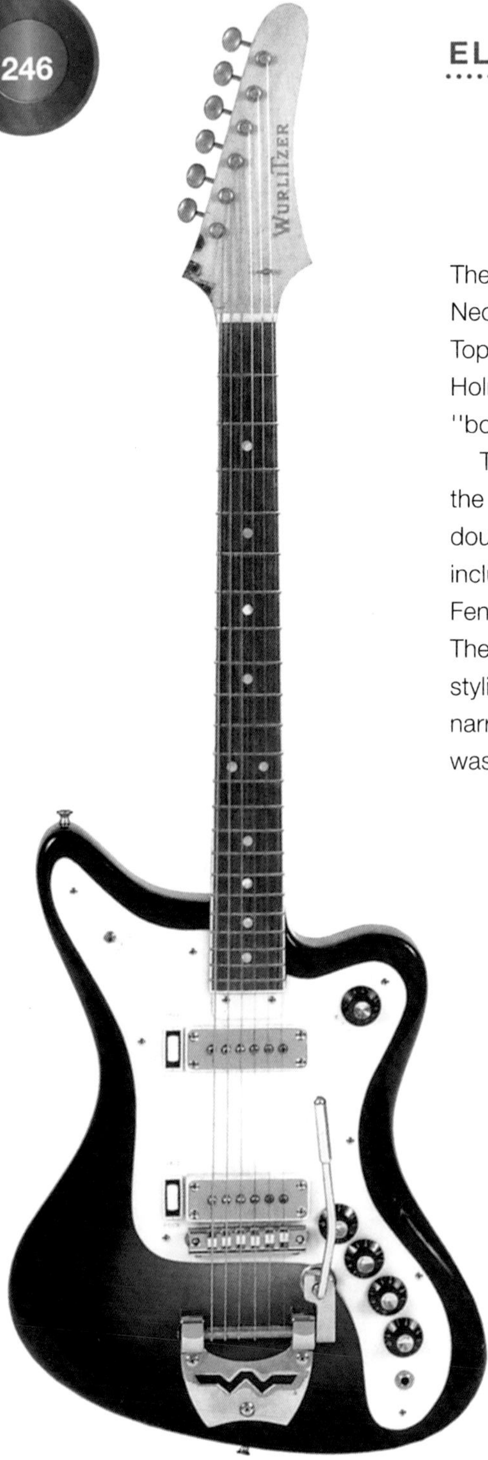

Wurlitzer Wildcat

The Holman-Woodell company, made this guitar in Neodesha, Kansas (around sixty miles due south from Topeka). The company also built their own brand, Holman, alongside the Wurlitzer models, and the famous "body-less" La Baye 2x4 guitars.

Three Wurlitzer models were produced, the Cougar, the Wildcat, and the Gemini. All were two-pickup offset double-cutaways with increasingly far-out styling, which included a six-in-line headstock. The Cougar was a Fender-style instrument, with a large, white pickguard. The Wildcat was a very similar guitar, except that its styling was even more exaggerated, and it had a narrower waist. Model 2520 was Taffy White, 2521 was Lollipop Red, and 2522 was Sunburst.

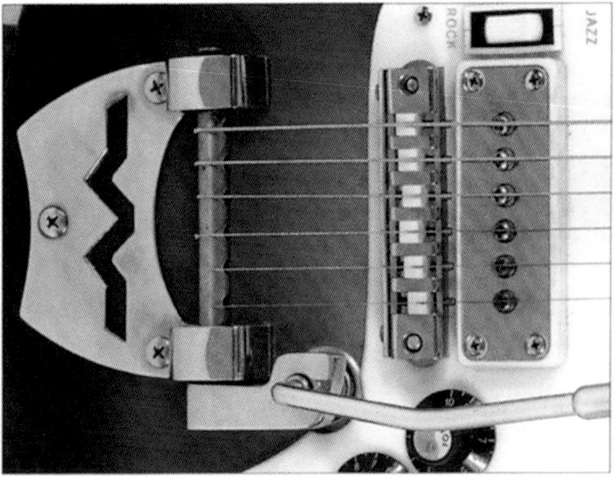

Here is a close-up of the Wildcat's Sensitone pickups, Tunemaster adjustable bridge, and "Wurlitzer Vibraton" vibrato (Wurlitzer's version of a Bigsby) with its W cutout in the base.

Yamaha Compass CPX15SA

The Yamaha CPX range of acoustics includes four themed instruments inspired by the points of the compass. The "south" model, finished in "Miami Ocean Blue," is intended to evoke a "tropical island paradise." Thanks to its "two-way" onboard electronics, boasting both a bridge saddle pickup and an internally mounted microphone, the guitar is sure to sound good in the often less than idyllic environment of a live gig, where any feedback can be eliminated by fitting a specially designed cover over its elegant soundhole.

The other three Compasses are equally striking: the "north" CPX boasts an "Arctic" finish, while its "east" and "west" cousins feature (respectively) Egyptian and Wild West motifs.

The CPX15SA's preamp allows outputs from its pickup and microphone to be combined.

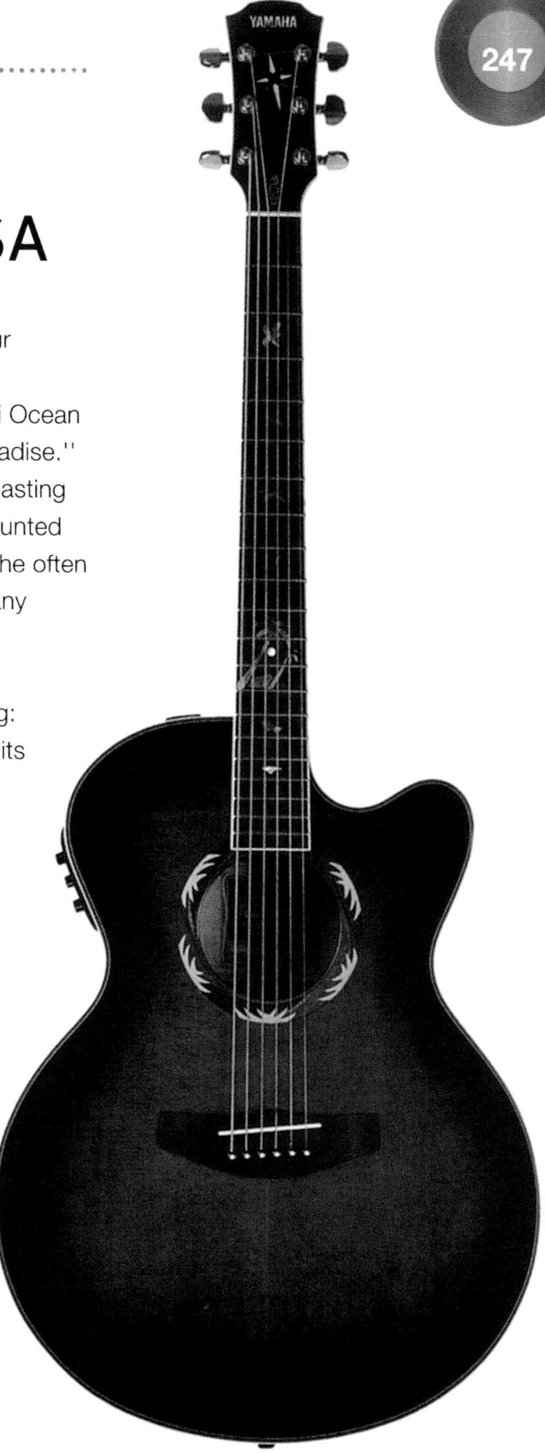

Yamaha Pacifica 112

In 1990, Yamaha launched its "Pacifica" range of solid-body electric guitars, "bred to perform in the most demanding musical situations." The instruments included both single- and double-cutaway designs, and were fitted with DiMarzio pickups. Rich Lasner, created them, he was a highly regarded music industry figure who had previously worked at Ibanez.

The Pacificas' bold styling and impressive specifications made them best sellers. The Pacifica 112 seen here has been widely recommended by reviewers and teachers as an ideal, relatively inexpensive beginner's guitar. Unusually for a cheaper axe, one of its three pickups is a humbucker. It also boasts a robust vibrato, alder body, and 22-fret maple neck.

Yamaha Pacifica 112 (with MIDI)

Like the Pacifica 112, Yamaha's more expensive Pacifica 912 is a highly versatile solid-body. It boasts three DiMarzio pickups, A PAF Pro at the bridge, and two Stratocaster-style HS-2s in the middle and neck positions. The previous owner of this instrument has taken his axe's capabilities even further by adding a synthesizer to interface with it.

The unit is a GK-2A made by the Japanese Roland Corporation. It enables signals from the Pacifica to be used to trigger sounds from external synths and samplers. This makes it possible for the guitar to sound like a trumpet, sax, or almost any other instrument, and it allows notes and chords to be recorded as MIDI (Musical Instrument Digital Interface) data.

This socket handles the output from both the Roland sensor and the Pacifica's DiMarzio pickups.

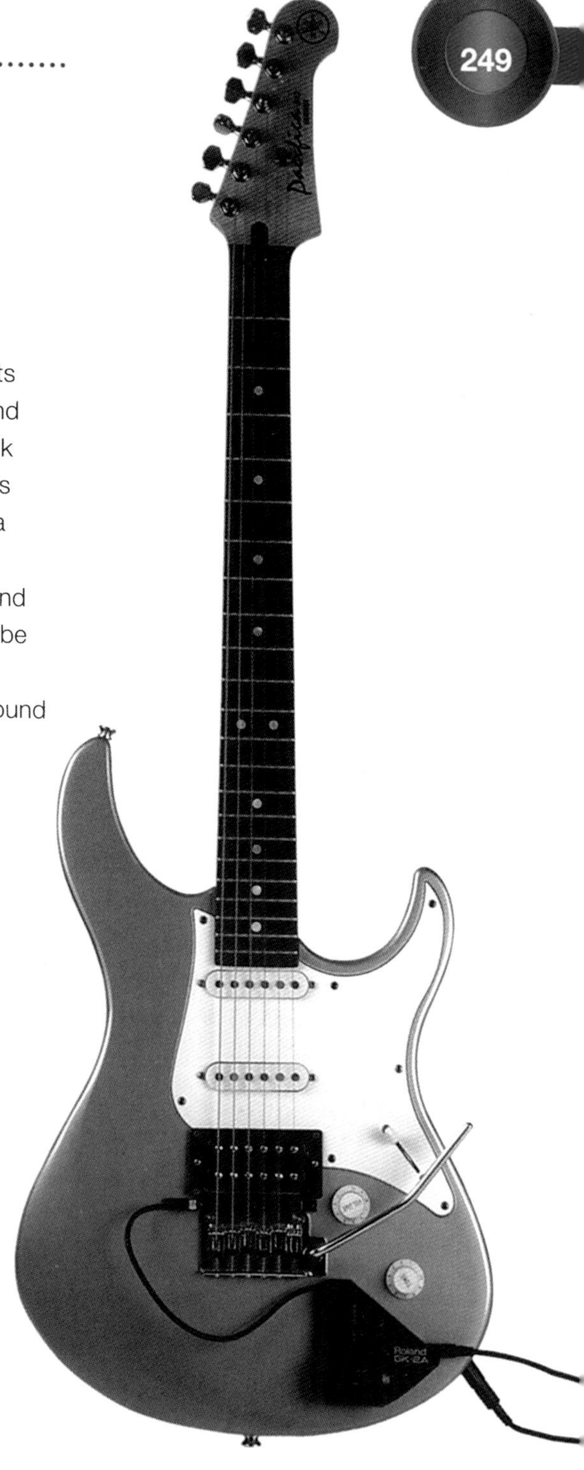

Yamaha SA500

Yamaha's "SA" (semi-acoustic) electric guitars were introduced in the early 1980s; they incorporate feedback-reducing, sustain-enhancing internal center blocks of the kind used by Gibson on its ES-335 and have proved enduringly popular.

The current "top of the line" SA is the SA2200, a maple-bodied model with an elegantly traditional look. It has now been joined by the less expensive SA500. The new instrument has a more contemporary appearance, thanks to its reshaped f-holes, and the provision of an "AES"-style tailpiece system (named for Yamaha's AES range of electrics) in place of the SA2200's more conventional "stud" unit. It has two humbucking pickups, and a sonokeling (rosewood) fingerboard.

This model lacks the more sophisticated pickup switching of the SA2200, which provides coil taps.

Yamaha SG500B

The "SG" line of solid-body electrics, launched in 1973-4 and discontinued in the late 1980s, played a crucial role in establishing Yamaha's international reputation among rock musicians. Carlos Santana became a keen used of two SG guitars: the SG-175, and the later SG-2000. Initially, the range included a handful of models with single-cutaway bodies that were slightly reminiscent of a Gibson Les Paul. But these were soon dropped, leaving the more famous double-cutaway outline (as seen on Santana's axes, and this SG500B) to establish itself as the classic Yamaha SG shape. The SG500B debuted in 1976 and remained in the catalog for about three years. This example dates from 1978, and is in almost mint condition.

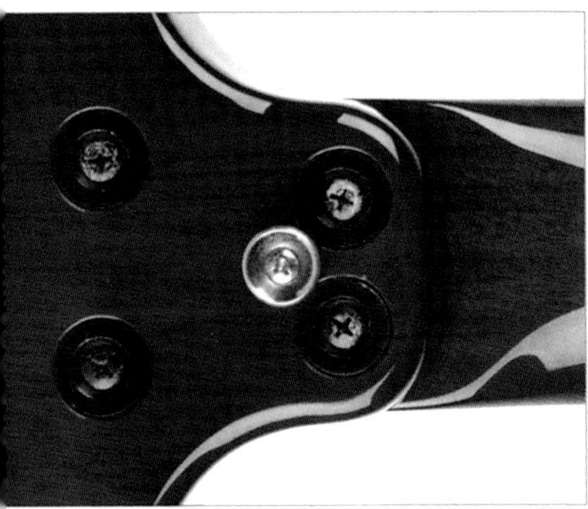

A detail of the guitar's back, where it joins the neck. The back and neck are made from mahogany and the screws secure the two parts together.

Yamaha TRB 6 II 6-String Bass

Yamaha's bass guitars are as highly respected as its standard acoustics and electrics. It produces over 40 models, including basses aimed at beginners and musicians on a tight budget, as well as state-of-the-art instruments endorsed by some of the leading names in rock and jazz. These included Nathan East, Billy Sheehan, Dave Santos, John Myung, and John Patitucci. Patitucci is a respected bandleader, soloist, composer, and teacher. He is closely associated with the TRB range, which Yamaha described as "the highest level of professional basses available for discriminating players." He currently uses a six-string TRB JP2, a signature version of this standard TRB 6 II. Both have twin Alnico V double-coil pickups.

The TRB 6 II's bridge, like the rest of its hardware, is machined from solid brass.

Zenith Super Cutaway

Boosey & Hawkes, a long-established British music publisher and retailer commissioned the German guitar maker, Framus, to produce a line of archtop acoustics in the early 1950s. They were branded with the name "Zenith." B&H enlisted top British jazz guitarist Ivor Mairants (1908-1998) to promote the guitars. He provided a warm endorsement for the Zeniths, stating that they "had a tone superior to any other at twice the price."

This guitar is Ivor's own, and is now on display at the Ivor Mairants Musicentre in London. He founded the store in 1962. Among the many Zenith players was Paul McCartney, who bought his at the age of 14, in a Liverpool department store in 1956.

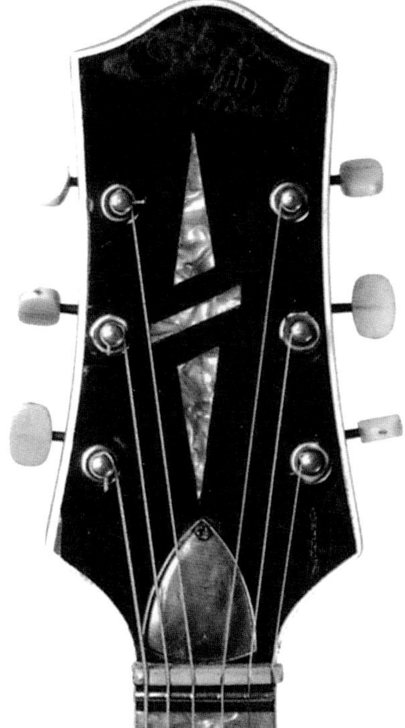

Index